WEEKEND MAKES

MACRAMÉ

25 QUICK AND EASY PROJECTS TO MAKE

WEEKEND MAKES

MACRAMÉ

25 QUICK AND EASY PROJECTS TO MAKE

STEPH BOOTH

First published 2021 by
Guild of Master Craftsman Publications Ltd Castle Place,
166 High Street, Lewes,
East Sussex, BN7 1XU

Text © Quail Publishing, 2021
Copyright in the Work © GMC Publications Ltd, 2021

ISBN 978-1-78494-619-7

A catalogue record for this book is available from
the British Library.

Project Manager: Kerry Kimber
Managing Art Editor: Darren Brant
Art Editor: Jennifer Stephens
Editors: Honor Head, Jean Coppendale
Technical Editor: Isabella Strambio
Photographer: Quail Studio
Stylist: Sarah Mosedale - Mose &

Colour origination by GMC Reprographics
Printed and bound in China

CONTENTS

INTRODUCTION

Macramé is a craft that uses a variety of knotting techniques to create textiles. I first came across macramé when I attended a workshop to make a bag. At the time I was trying out a variety of different crafts and was enjoying being creative with new skills. I immediately took to macramé. Working with fibres and watching them grow with every row of knots is very rewarding, and I love the variety of home and wardrobe accessories that can be made.

Macramé started as the creative art of knot tying in the 13th century and enjoyed a resurgence of popularity in the 1970s. Now, it is once more back in vogue, with designers and crafters using it to bring warm textures and organic structures into the home. It's exciting to see how macramé is being adapted into a more contemporary style, helped greatly by the wide availability of materials and tools that enable us to create incredible pieces of macramé art and beautiful homeware.

Crafting has long been associated with mindfulness, and for me, macramé is the perfect activity to promote relaxation and a sense of well-being. The rhythm of knotting is almost meditative, and the joy of creating something from nothing is very rewarding.

It's a delight to feature alongside the other talented artists within this book and to have this opportunity to share our creative ideas with you. The book provides a range of designs using a variety of knots and skills, so whether you are a complete beginner or you're keen to improve your techniques, you'll discover many projects in these pages that will inspire you to be creative with macramé.

Steph Booth

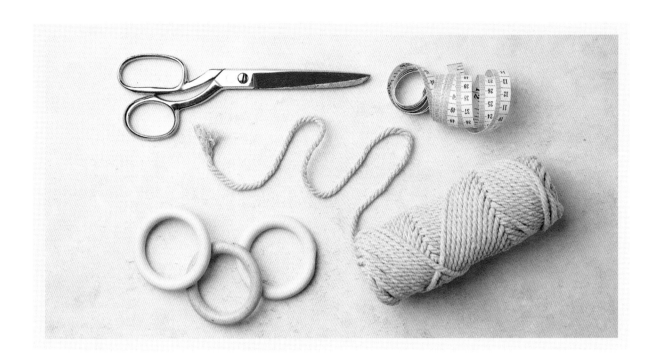

TOOLS AND MATERIALS

CORDS

The projects usually specify the length and type of cord required. Common materials include cotton, hemp, polyester and jute. 'Braided' cords are less likely to fray, while 'twisted' cords fray easily. Twisted cord can be made up of a single strand (or 'ply') or several strands twisted together. For example, 3-ply cord consists of three strands. When choosing a cord, consider whether fraying ends are desirable for the project you've chosen, or something you want to avoid. The scale of the project will dictate the thickness of the cord you should use. Fine cord will create intricate work, while chunky rope is ideal for dramatic artworks.

RINGS

Rings made from metal or wood are often used to hang macramé, perhaps as a wall hanging or plant hanger. They are also sometimes used as handles for bags. Rings are available in a variety of sizes.

HOOPS

Hoops can be used as a frame for macramé, with the cords being tied in and around the edges of the hoop as you work.

DOWELS

Lengths of wood or a sturdy stick or branch can be used for macramé wall hangings.

BEADS

Beads, charms and other decorations can be added to macramé projects by threading them onto the cord as you work. Check that the hole through the middle is at least the same width as the thickness of the cord you are using.

S-HOOKS

These 'S' shaped metal hooks are ideal for hanging macramé projects while you work. They can be hooked over a clothes rail, curtain rail, towel rail or the back of a chair.

ADJUSTABLE CLOTHES RAIL WITH WHEELS

While not essential, an adjustable, portable clothes rail can be really helpful for hanging macramé projects at a comfortable height while you work. The wheels also offer the extra convenience of allowing you to store your work or move it around.

MASKING TAPE

Use tape to prevent the ends of cords from fraying, and to mark straight edges before trimming the cord ends.

HAIRSPRAY OR SPRAY-ON STARCH

You can use a light mist of hairspray or spray-on starch to keep tassels and fringing in place once your project is complete and ready to hang.

CROCHET HOOK OR TAPESTRY NEEDLE

A hook or needle is helpful for pulling cord through knots or beads, and for sewing in ends.

TAPE MEASURE

A measuring tape is an essential piece of equipment as cords need to be measured and cut to exact lengths at the start of a project.

SHARP SCISSORS

Sharp fabric scissors will make cutting thick cords easier and allow for neat, trimmed edges.

COMB OR PET BRUSH

These can be used to create a frayed effect on the ends of cords.

DRESSMAKERS' PINS

These can be used to hold cords in place.

COMMON MACRAMÉ TERMS

ALTERNATING:
Switching between cords to create a row of knots.

BUNDLE:
Grouping together a set of cords to help separate or organise them.

CROOK:
The curved edge of a loop.

DIAGONAL:
A sequence of diagonal knots.

FILLER CORD:
One or more cords that remain in the middle of the design with knots wrapped around them.

FINISHING KNOT:
A knot tied to secure the ends of the cords to prevent them from becoming loose and unravelling.

FRINGE:
A decorative feature of long, loose cords at the base of a project.

HOLDING (GUIDE) CORD:
One or more cords that hold the knots made by working cords.

PICOT:
Loops that stand out on the edges of the design.

ROW:
A sequence of horizontal knots.

SINNET:
A chain of knots.

WEAVE:
Cords that alternately cross over and under one another.

WORKING CORD:
The cord you are using to tie knots.

KNOTS AND TECHNIQUES

LARK'S HEAD KNOT

The lark's head knot is used to attach cords to a dowel or holding cord. It has a horizontal bump facing towards you.

1 Fold the cord in half and place the loop behind and below the dowel/holding cord.

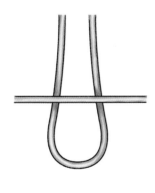

2 Pass the cord ends through the loop. Pull the cord ends to tighten the knot.

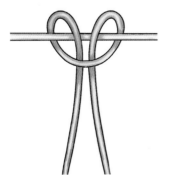

REVERSE LARK'S HEAD KNOT

The reverse lark's head knot is the same as the lark's head knot, except the horizontal bump is at the back.

1 Fold the cord in half and place the loop behind and above the dowel/holding cord.

2 Pass the cord ends through the loop. Pull the cord ends to tighten the knot.

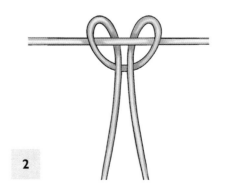

VERTICAL LARK'S HEAD KNOT

The vertical lark's head knot is a variation of the lark's head knot.

1 Take the working cord around the vertical dowel or filler cord and bring it back to the front, over the top of itself.

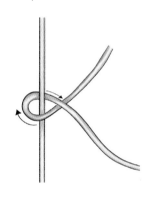

2 Pass the cord under the filler below, then over the top of the filler and then under the vertical line created by itself. Pull the cord ends to tighten the knot.

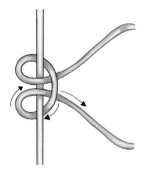

OVERHAND KNOT

An overhand knot is the simplest way of tying a knot.

Create a loop and pass the end through from back to front. Pull the cord ends to tighten the knot.

HALF KNOT

A half knot is the first half of a square knot (see right). Worked with four cords, half knots can be tied in alternating directions to create a straight cord, or they can be repeated in the same direction to create a twisted cord, sometimes known as a spiral knot.

1 The outside cords are working cords and the inside cords are filler cords. Take the first working cord and pass it under the last working cord.

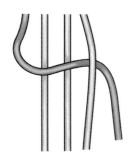

2 Now take the last working cord and bring it under the two filler cords, and back up and over the first working cord.

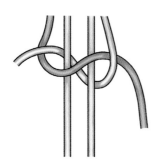

SQUARE KNOT

A standard square knot uses four cords. It can be left or right facing, depending on whether you start making the knot with the working cord on the left or the right.

1 The outside cords are working cords and the inside cords are filler cords. Take the first working cord and pass it under the last working cord.

2 Now take the last working cord and bring under the two filler cords and back up, and over the first working cord (continued overleaf).

3 Bring the first working cord back over the filler cords and under the last working cord.

3

4 Take the last working cord and pass it under the filler cords and back up between the second filler cord and the first working cord.

Pull the working cords to tighten the knot and keep the filler cords straight.

4

SWITCH KNOT

The switch knot is worked with four cords and is often used to create a lacy, decorative effect.

1 Create a square knot (see page 13).

1

2 Create a second square knot further down the work, using the filler cords from the first square knot as the working cords.

2

3 Continue making square knots in this way, switching filler and working cords when each knot is completed.

3

HALF HITCH KNOT

Half hitch knots can be tied horizontally, vertically or diagonally using the working cord and the holding or filler cord. It is the first step of the double half hitch knot.

Wrap the working cord around the filler cord and then pass the end through the loop to secure.

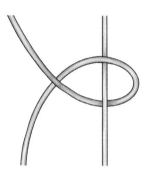

DOUBLE HALF HITCH (CLOVE HITCH) KNOT

A double half hitch knot, also known as the clove hitch, is where two half hitch knots are worked, one after the other.

Wrap the working cord around the filler cord, then pass the end through the loop created by the working cord. Repeat this once more and gently pull to secure.

A reverse double half hitch is the same as shown above, except the cord is wrapped around the filler cord from the right hand side.

BERRY KNOT

This sculptural knot may be used once, or repeated across a panel to create a textured pattern.

1 Start by making a number of square knots (see page 13). This will be noted in your project instructions as a sinnet.

2 Leaving the working cords hanging at the sides, bring the ends of the filler cords up and pass them between the two fillers above the sinnet, from the front to the back. Pull them down so that the sinnet curls up to form a berry shape.

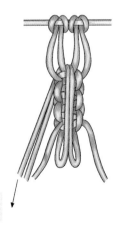

3 Tie a half or full square knot below to fasten.

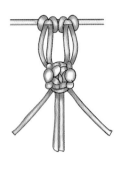

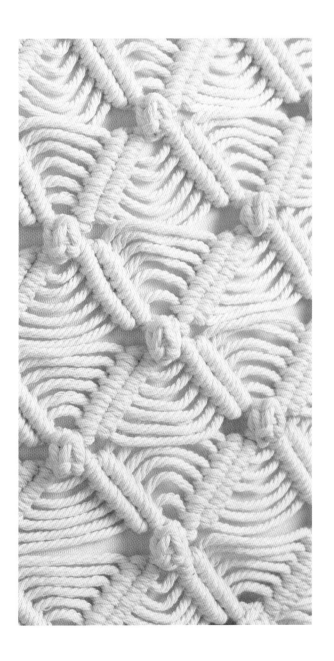

WRAP KNOT

The wrap knot (sometimes called a gathering knot) is commonly used to secure cords together. It's created by wrapping a working cord around filler cords.

1 Create a loop in the working cord and wrap the end around the filler cords, starting from the top and working down.

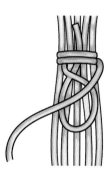

1

2 Stop wrapping at your desired length and pass the working cord through the loop.

2

3 Pull the working cord tight. Trim any excess cord as desired.

3

DIAGONAL DOUBLE HALF HITCH KNOT

In a diagonal double half hitch knot, a diagonal line is created by working the knots a little lower each time.

1 Using the cord at the edge as the filler cord, hold it diagonally across the work. Use the next cord as the working cord to create the first double half hitch knot (see page 15).

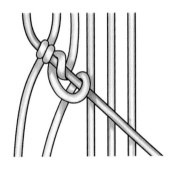

2 Continue working left to right, with each double half hitch slightly lower than the previous one to create the diagonal line. Return in the other direction to create a zigzag line.

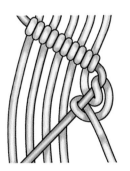

VERTICAL DOUBLE HALF HITCH KNOT

In a vertical double half hitch knot, the vertical cords are used as filler cords and the same working cord is used across the row.

1 Starting with the cord on the left as your first filler cord, make a half hitch knot (see page 15) around it with the working cord.

2 Repeat Step 1 to add another knot directly underneath the first, passing the end through the loop.

3 Repeat Steps 1 and 2 across all the filler cords.

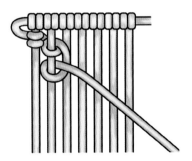

HORIZONTAL DOUBLE HALF HITCH KNOT

The horizontal double half hitch knot is created by working around a horizontal filler cord and moving left to right or right to left.

1 Using the cord on the left as the filler cord, hold it horizontally across the front of the panel. Use the next cord along as the first working cord. Bring it forwards, under the filler cord, then up and over the filler cord towards the left.

2 Wrap the working cord around the filler cord to the right. Pull the end through the loop under the filler cord.

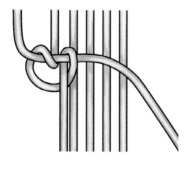

3 Repeat Steps 1 and 2 with the next cord along.

RYA KNOT

Rya knots can be used to make tassels or fringing.

1 Take one or more cords and hold them horizontally in front of the vertical cords. Wrap the ends backwards around two cords and then bring them forwards, in between the same two cords.

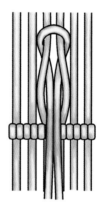

2 Pull to tighten the knot.

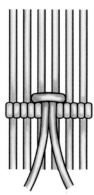

BARREL KNOT

The barrel knot is created with one cord and is often used as a finishing knot at the ends of cords to prevent them from unravelling.

1 Make a loop with the working cord.

2 Wrap the end around itself, within the loop.

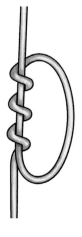

3 Hold the cord at the top and bottom, gently pulling to tighten the knot.

PIPA KNOT

The pipa knot is often used to create a decorative pendant.

1 Fold a length of cord in half and place the right cord over the left to create a loop.

2 Use the right cord to create a figure of eight. Take the right cord behind the centre twist.

3 Bring the right cord over the front and down, looping it inside the previous bottom loop.

4 Take the right cord around the back, behind the centre twist.

5 Bring the right cord over the front and down, looping it inside the previous bottom loop.

6 Repeat Steps 4 and 5 until the bottom of the figure of eight is filled. To finish, place the working end through the middle hole from the front to the back.

FEATHER KNOT

Feather knots can be used individually to make accessories and decorations, or they can be added to a project to create layered fringing.

1 Measure out some cords according to the project instructions. Fold the first cord in half and place it at a right angle under the filler cords with the loop on the right.

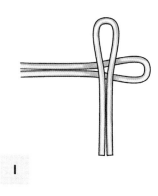

2 Fold another cord in half and pass the loop up from the back to the front, and through the loop of the first cord.

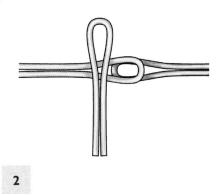

3 Pass the ends of the first cord up through the loop of the second cord, from the back to the front.

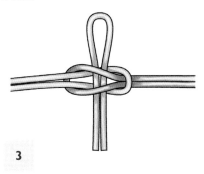

4 Pull tight to secure.

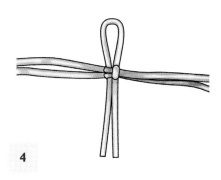

5 Repeat Steps 1 to 4, alternately reversing the direction of the cords.

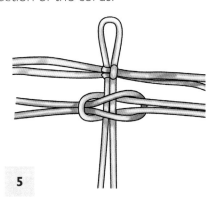

6 Trim to shape, and brush to fray the edges (see page 25).

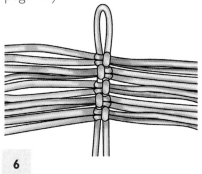

TURK'S HEAD KNOT

Made with a variable number of interwoven cords, they can be tied flat or around a column.

1 Make two loops, one on top of each other, and then create a third loop by weaving the cord over, under and over.

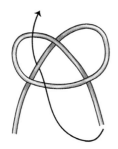

2 To create a fourth loop, weave the cord under, over, under and over.

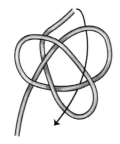

3 To create the final loop, join the ends.

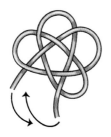

CROWN KNOT

The crown knot may be used individually to finish off a macramé piece, or it may be repeated to form a textured cord or sinnet.

1 Hold four cords at right angles to each other.

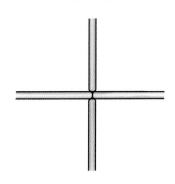

2 Take the first cord and pass it over the next cord, creating a loop. Take the second cord and pass it around and over the first and third cord.

3 Take the third cord and fold it over the second and fourth cords. Pass the fourth cord over the third and the first cord and pull through the loop created by the first cord.

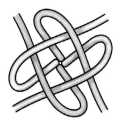

4 Gently pull each cord, one at a time, to tighten the knot.

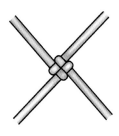

FINISHING TECHNIQUES

FRAYING

To create fringing, untwist the cords to separate out the individual strands.

BRUSHING

For a soft finish to your fringing, fray the ends and then use a pet brush or comb to brush and separate the individual strands on both sides of the work. Mist with water and lay flat to dry. Finish with a light spray of hairspray or spray-on starch to keep the fringing looking neat.

TRIMMING

Once the fringing has been frayed or brushed, place a strip of masking tape to indicate the cutting line. Then use sharp fabric or embroidery scissors to cut a neat edge.

SEWING IN ENDS

Loose ends of cord can be woven into the back of your work using a blunt, large-eyed sewing needle or a tapestry needle.

SIMPLE PLANT HANGER

DESIGNED BY LISA MILLER

Introduce more greenery into your house with the help of a simple but effective plant hanger. These hanging homes for houseplants are perfect for when you've run out of shelf space, and this beginner's pattern is a great way to practise your newly learned macramé knots.

SKILL LEVEL: EASY

YOU'LL NEED

- 1in (3cm) diameter wooden ring
- 31yd (28.3m) of ⅛in (3mm) cord in natural
- 6 × ¼in (12mm) wooden beads
- Tape measure
- Sharp scissors
- Masking tape

KNOTS AND TECHNIQUES

- Wrap knot
- Square knot
- Half knot

PREPARATION

Cut the following lengths of cord:

6 × 15ft (4.5m)

2 × 17in (43cm)

FINISHED SIZE

Length: approximately 32in (82cm)

Pot size: approximately 4¼in (11cm) in diameter

METHOD

1 Feed all six lengths of 15ft (4.5m) cord through the wooden ring, until the cord is in half. Take one of the 17in (43cm) cords and make a wrap knot (see page 17) to secure the cords onto the ring.

2 Separate the cords into three groups of four strands of cord.

3 Take one of the groups and tie 6in (15cm) of square knots (see page 13) and repeat for the remaining two groups.

4 Take the outer two cords from each of the three groups and thread a wooden bead onto each. This should leave you with two wooden beads at the end of each square knot section. Placing a small piece of tape on the ends of the cord may help you to thread the beads onto the cord.

5 Leave a small 1in (2cm) gap to allow for the bead, and then tie 6in (15cm) of half knots (see page 13) onto each group, creating spirals.

6 Drop down 6in (15cm) and gather two outer pieces of cord from neighbouring groups and make one square knot. Repeat this for each group so that you have three square knots, 6in (15cm) down from the rest of your design.

7 Drop down 3in (7cm) and gather four cords from your original groups and make another square knot. Repeat this for the remaining cords.

8 Take your final piece of 17in (43cm) cord and tie a wrap knot approximately 1in (2cm) below your final square knots.

9 Trim the cord to your preference (I like mine quite long) and your hanger is finished!

Tip

This design is just a guide; feel free to experiment with different knot patterns and beads to create a variety of styles.

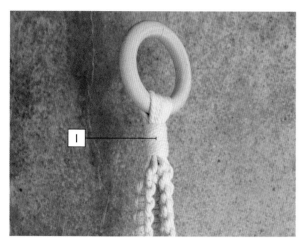

CUSHION

DESIGNED BY LUCY BOOTH

This beautiful macramé cushion is an ideal way to bring extra personality to your interiors. From living room to bedroom or office, this eye-catching geometric design will become the focal point of any room. Style it with other inspirational pieces such as macramé coasters or wall hangings to make your living space chic and on-trend.

SKILL LEVEL: REQUIRES EXPERIENCE

YOU'LL NEED

- 19in (48cm) long (at least) wooden dowel rod to attach cords to while you work
- 19in (48cm) square plain canvas cushion cover
- 218yd (200m) of ⅛in (3mm) 3-ply twisted cord in natural
- Tape measure
- Sharp scissors
- Dressmakers' pins
- Sewing needle and thread
- Comb

KNOTS AND TECHNIQUES

- Lark's head knot
- Double half hitch knot
- Diagonal double half hitch knot
- Horizontal double half hitch knots
- Berry knot
- Wrap knot
- Fraying
- Brushing

PREPARATION

Cut the following lengths of cord:

40 × 14½ft (4.4m)

FINISHED SIZE

Length: 19in (48cm)

Width: 19in (48cm)

METHOD

1 Attach all 40 cords to the dowel rod one at a time using the lark's head knot (see page 11) and pull tight. Double check that the width of the total knots on the rod sits within the width of the cushion cover.

2 Before starting the design, leave a gap of a few inches (about 7cm) between the dowel and where you will start working. This will be used to create the tassels at the top of the cushion.

3 Make a horizontal line of double half hitch knots (see page 15), using all 40 cords.

4 Create a second line of double half hitch knots under the first.

5 Continue using the double half hitch knot to create the next part of the design. Using eight cords, create a line of diagonal double half hitch knots (see page 18) down the right side, from left to right. Repeat to create a second row of diagonal double half hitch knots directly underneath the first.

6 Take the next eight cords and repeat Step 5, but work diagonally down to the left, from right to left, to meet the row you have just created in the middle.

7 To secure the diagonal rows of double half hitch knots together, use the four middle cords to make a berry knot (see page 16).

8 Repeat Steps 5 and 6 to create the bottom half of the 'flower' shape. Make two lines of diagonal double half hitch knots, but this time work the rows in Step 5 from right to left; and the rows in Step 6, from left to right. You have now made the first flower shape.

9 Repeat the same process using all the cords and creating a row of five flowers. The bottom of the first row of flowers will become the top of the second row and so on. You should complete eight rows in total, alternating between five and four rows of flowers.

10 Once you have finished the flowers, add two lines of horizontal double half hitch knots (see page 19). Then slide the work off the end of the dowel rod. Cut each loop to the length you want your tassels to be.

11 Fold your macramé horizontally, bringing the bottom up to the top, and trim the cords at the bottom of the design to the same length as those at the top.

12 Place the design on top of your cushion cover, pinning it in place. Open the zip on the cushion cover so you can get your hand inside. Take your needle and thread and sew between the top two rows and bottom two rows of double half hitch knots to secure your piece in place.

13 Take the hanging cords from the piece and gather up 20 cords at a time and secure them with a wrap knot (see page 17). Continue to do this with every 20 cords. You should end up with four tassels at both top and bottom.

14 Once all the tassels are secured, carefully brush or comb out the ends of the remaining cords to complete the 'frayed' tassel look (see page 25).

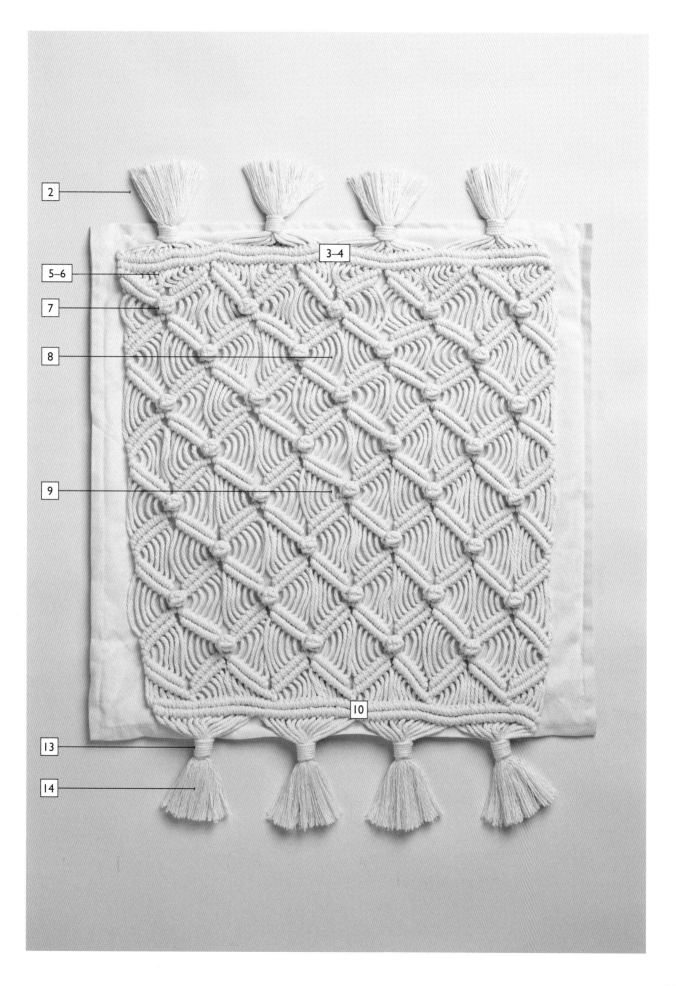

MAKE-UP BAG

DESIGNED BY LUCY BOOTH

Stylish and practical, this macramé bag is just right for carrying all your small essentials. Fill it with make-up, toiletries, sunglasses, spare change, or anything else you need to take with you on your travels. The striking design can be enhanced with a decorative tassel, which will also provide easy access to your belongings.

SKILL LEVEL: REQUIRES EXPERIENCE

YOU'LL NEED

- 6¼in x 8¾ (16 x 22cm) plain cosmetic liner bag with zip fastening

- 218yd (200m) of ⅛in (3mm) cord in natural

- Tape measure

- Sharp scissors

- Dressmakers' pins

- Sewing needle and thread

KNOTS AND TECHNIQUES

- Reverse lark's head knot

- Double half hitch knot

- Square knot

- Wrap knot

- Overhand knot

PREPARATION

Cut the following lengths of cord:

32 x 12ft (3.6m)

1 x 4¾ft (1.5m)

FINISHED SIZE

Length: 9in (23cm)

Width: 6¾in (17cm)

METHOD

1 Attach a 12ft (360cm) cord to the 4¾ft (150cm) cord by making a reverse lark's head knot (see page 11) or, if you find it easier to make, a standard lark's head knot.

2 Repeat with all of the 12ft (360cm) cords, adding each cord one at time.

3 Begin by making a row of square knots (see page 13) using all the cords. Then tie a row of alternating square knots, putting aside the first two and last two cords (see page 10).

4 Continue until you have made five rows of alternating square knots.

5 To create the triangles, continue to make square knots, leaving the cords from the first three square knots and working with the cords from the next five square knots. Work underneath them and create another four square knots. Then create three more square knots under that row. The sequence to create is 5–4–3–2–1.

6 Moving along to the next triangle, repeat the same process. Count five square knots and work underneath these to create four more. Continue the 5–4–3–2–1 sequence. Leave the cords from the last three square knots, as you did with the first three in Step 5.

7 Now go back and work with the cords from the three square knots you left out in Step 5. A different sequence is needed here. Using the alternating rule, work on a diagonal to create the sequence 3–2–2–1–1. By continuing this process, you are still producing the little loops.

8 Repeat Step 7 with the cords from the three square knots you left out in Step 6, using the same sequence.

9 Make a diagonal line of double half hitch knots (see page 15) to frame the square knots you've just made.

10 Once you've created the top half of the triangle, secure all the cords in the middle of the triangle using a large square knot aligned with the ends of the double half hitch lines. Use the first and last cord as working cords and the remaining as filler cords.

11 Repeat Step 9 to create two more square knot triangles.

12 Tie a square knot at the end of the diagonal double half hitch lines.

13 Continue to create a single line of double half hitch knots to fully frame all the triangles.

14 Make another line of double half hitch knots, just on the bottom half.

15 The bottom of the diamonds will now be the top of the next diamonds. Secure all the cords by tying a large square knot in the middle, aligned with the ends of the lines of double half hitch. Use the first and last cords as working cords and the remaining as filler cords.

16 At the end of the diagonal lines of double half hitch knots tie a square knot.

17 Close the diamond shapes with diagonal lines of double half hitch knots.

18 Starting from the left, take the first four cords and tie a square knot. Continue making rows of alternating square knots until you are aligned with the bottom of the diamond shapes.

19 Repeat the same alternating square knots pattern on the other side and in between the diamonds.

20 Make 23 more rows of square knots, using the alternating pattern.

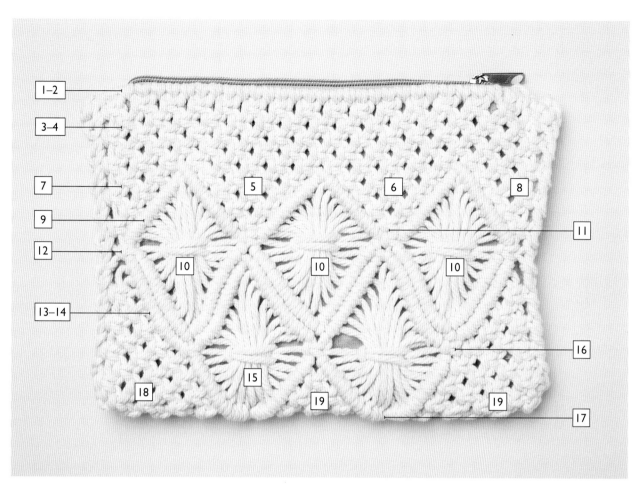

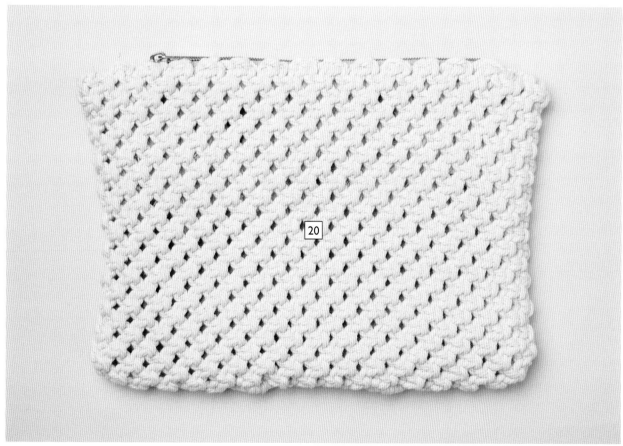

21 Before continuing, make sure the cosmetic bag will fit within the macrame – ideally, the macrame should be ⅛in larger all the way around. Cut off the excess cord, leaving just a few inches (about 7cm). These will be tucked in, so they won't be seen.

22 Fold the bag in half, placing the liner bag in the middle. Line up the tops so you can check that the liner bag fits inside. Pin the macramé bag together around the liner bag to ensure it fits. Then remove the liner, ready for the next step.

23 Now, thread the holding cord that you used to secure all the cords in the beginning through the small loops on either side of the bag to sew up the side seams. Push the liner back inside the bag and pin it in place before sewing it in using a needle and thread. Technically, this is the end of the project. However, if you would like to add a macramé tassel to the zip fastening of your bag, continue with the next steps (right).

MACRAMÉ TASSEL

1 Take 28 of the end cords you cut off in Step 21. Measure them out to 12in (30.5cm) long.

2 Take 25 of those cords and lay them out next to each other on a hard and stable surface.

3 Now, take one more cord, fold in half and make a double overhand knot (see page 12) about halfway down, to create a loop, before cutting off the excess end. The longer or bigger the loop, the further the tassel will hang down outside the bag. I recommend keeping it to roughly halfway for the ideal size.

4 Now, take the looped cord and place it in the middle of the 25 cords. Make sure the overhand knot is hidden within the cords.

5 Take the last cord and place it perpendicularly, under all the existing cords, in the middle. Take one end of the cord, pass it through the looped cord and then tie a double overhand knot over all the cords, pulling it tight. This ensures that the knotted looped end cannot go past that cord and come loose. Once you have secured the cord with a knot, trim off the excess ends.

6 Grab the loop at the top and you'll see that all the cords are hanging down and hiding the tied cord in the centre. Shuffle some of the cords around if you can see the cords underneath.

7 Hang your tassel from a hook, and use both hands to secure a wrap knot (see page 17). This will complete the tassel.

8 To finish off, attach the tassel to the zip fastening using a reverse lark's head knot. Pull it tight so it is secure.

WALL HANGING

DESIGNED BY ISABELLA STRAMBIO

With its dense texture, flowy fringing, sharp angles and contrasting colours, this modern macramé wall hanging will make a stunning standout piece for any home.

SKILL LEVEL: REQUIRES EXPERIENCE

YOU'LL NEED

- 23½in (60cm) long wooden dowel rod or stick
- 100yd (92m) of ¼in (5mm) single twist cotton cord in natural
- 57¾yd (53m) of ¼in (5mm) single twist cotton cord in teal
- Tape measure
- Sharp scissors
- Tapestry needle

KNOTS AND TECHNIQUES

- Lark's head knot
- Square knot
- Double half hitch knot
- Vertical double half hitch knot

PREPARATION

Cut the following lengths of natural cord:

10 x 78in (2m)

16 x 3½yd (3m)

6 x 3¾yd (3.6m)

2 x 39in (1m)

Cut the following lengths of teal cord:

12 x 78in (2m)

5 x 57in (1.5m)

15 x 48in (1.3m)

2 x 39in (1m)

FINISHED SIZE

Length: approximately 38in (96.5cm), excluding the dowel

Width: approximately 15in (38cm)

METHOD

1 Tie 32 natural cords onto the dowel rod using lark's head knots (see page 11). Work from left to right. First, tie the 78in (2m) long cords, then the 3½yd (3m) and finally the 3¾yd (3.6m).

2 Starting from the left, make nine rows of alternating square knots (see page 13), ending with a line of 16 square knots.

3 Next, put aside the first two cords on the left and make a line of 15 square knots.

4 Continue by putting aside the first two cords every time you start a new row of square knots, until you have 39 rows of alternating square knots in total, and the last row only has one square knot.

5 Use one 39in (1m) natural cord as a guide cord, and tie a diagonal line of double half hitch knots (see page 15) with all your cords, working from left to right.

6 Use the second 39in (1m) natural cord as a second guide cord and tie another line of double half hitch knots with all your cords, working from left to right. Add the guide cord from Step 5 on the diagonal line of double half hitch knots.

7 Starting from the left, put aside the two ends of the guide cords and the first cord from the diagonal line of double half hitch knots.

8 Take the first 78in (2m) long teal cord, and tie a vertical double half hitch knot (see page 18) onto the second and third natural cords, making sure the two ends of the teal cord are equal in length.

9 Continue tying the 78in (2m) long cords onto two natural colour cords at the same time.

10 Once you have tied all the 78in (2m) long teal cords, tie the 57in (1.5m) long teal cords and then the 48in (1.3m) long teal cords, tying them onto two natural cords at the same time, as in Step 9.

11 Use a 39in (1m) teal cord as a guide cord, and tie a diagonal line of double half hitch knots with all the teal cords, working from left to right.

12 Use the last 39in (1m) cord as a second guide cord and tie another diagonal line of double half hitch knots with all your cords, working from left to right. Add the guide cord from Step 11 onto the diagonal line of double half hitch knots.

13 Measure the height of the nine rows of alternating square knots at the top left (it should be approximately 4–5in [10–12cm]), and cut the last teal cord on the right to match.

14 Cut the rest of the cords, mirroring the angle of the double half hitch knots, to create the fringing.

15 Turn your macramé over, so that the wrong side is facing up, and trim the guide cords and all the natural cords to about 2in (5cm) and, with the help of a tapestry needle, tuck them behind one or two knots.

Tips

You can be playful with the colours for this project and use different coloured cords that complement the scheme of your interior. You could also make a pair of wall hangings by swapping the colours and mirroring the pattern.

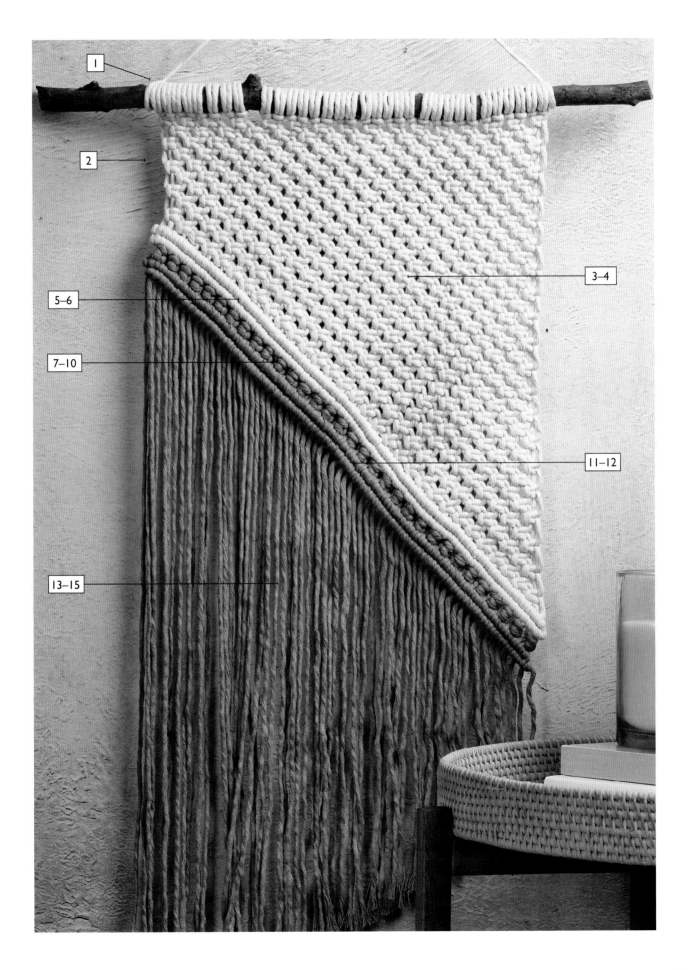

BRACELET
DESIGNED BY ABI WILLIAMS

Tie an outfit together the natural way with this beautiful bohemian-style cuff, the perfect addition to your accessory collection. Featuring a triple diamond design and edged with a soft brushed fringe, the bracelet is made from natural cotton and finished with a leather cord fastening.

SKILL LEVEL: REQUIRES EXPERIENCE

YOU'LL NEED

- 6in (15cm) long (at least) wooden dowel rod to attach cords to while you work
- 21½yd (19.6m) of ¹⁄₁₆in (1.5mm) single twist cotton cord in natural
- 44in (112cm) flat suede leather cord
- Tape measure
- Sharp scissors
- Comb

KNOTS AND TECHNIQUES

- Lark's head knot
- Square knot
- Double half hitch knot
- Fraying
- Brushing

PREPARATION

Cut the following lengths of natural cord:

16 × 16in (40.5cm)

2 × 32in (82cm)

FINISHED SIZE

Length: approximately 5½in (14cm)

Width: approximately 3in (7cm)

METHOD

1 Attach the 16 lengths of 16in (40.5cm) long cord to the dowel rod, using lark's head knots (see page 11). Taking the two longer lengths of cord (32in [82cm]), attach one to the dowel at either end of the 16 lengths, also using lark's head knots.

2 Make a row of double half hitch knots (see page 15) along the top.

3 Working from left to right, tie two square knots (see page 13) alongside each other. Skip the next four cords, then tie one square knot. Skip the next four cords, then tie one square knot. Skip the next four cords, then tie two square knots.

4 On the next row, between the first two square knots, tie one square knot. Repeat on the right-hand side.

5 Using the first four loose cords from the top row, create the top half of your first diamond using the double half hitch knot.

6 In the middle of each diamond, tie a square knot, leaving the outside cords of the diamond free. Finish off the bottom half of each of the diamonds, using the double half hitch knot.

7 Tie a square knot in between the bottom part of the diamonds (to mirror the top half of the cuff).

8 Finish off both sides with alternating square knots until they are level with the bottom of the diamonds.

9 Make a horizontal row of double half hitch knots.

10 Take the piece off the wooden dowel. Tie an overhand knot (see page 12) in the top left cord and the bottom right cord to stop the piece from moving.

11 Trim the top and bottom of the cords to approximately 1in (2.5cm). Brush or comb the cords out, until they are feathery and fluffy (see page 25). Once brushed, you can trim them again to neaten.

12 To attach the cord for fastening, thread it through the loops created by the square knots in a criss-cross pattern. Tie the cord in a bow to fasten.

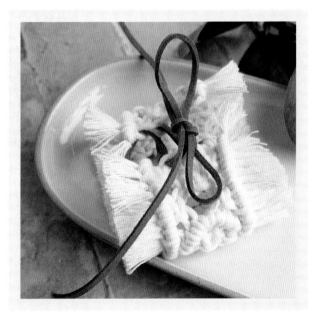

Tip

Instead of using suede leather cord for the fastening, you can use more macramé cord or ribbon.

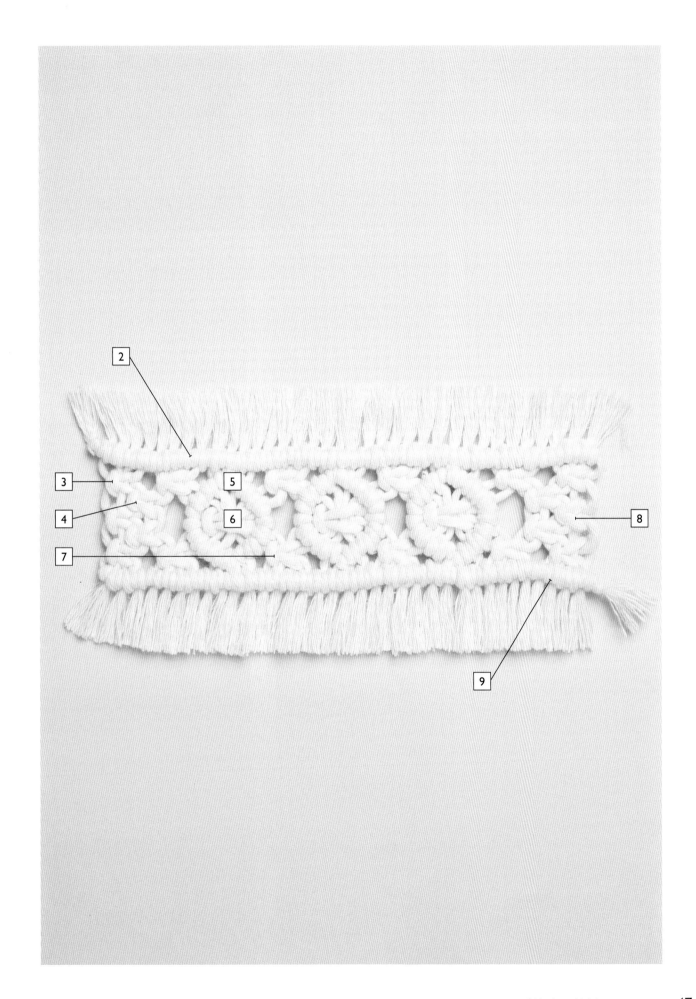

LAMPSHADE

DESIGNED BY HANNAH MCVIE

This beautifully handcrafted lampshade will give any room the wow factor. Elegant and textural, it may look complicated, but this statement shade is simple to create and can be adapted to suit your individual style.

SKILL LEVEL: EASY

YOU'LL NEED

- Adjustable clothes rail or wooden dowel rod and S-hooks to hang lampshade from while you work
- 30in (76cm) lampshade frame
- 76½yd (70m) of ¼in (5mm) single twist cord in natural
- 15yd (14m) of ¼in (5mm) single twist cord in beige
- Tape measure
- Sharp scissors
- Comb

KNOTS AND TECHNIQUES

- Lark's head knot
- Double half hitch knot
- Diagonal double half hitch knot
- Fraying
- Brushing
- Rya knot

PREPARATION

Cut the following lengths of natural cord:

69 x 40in (100cm)

Cut the following lengths of beige cord:

54 x 10in (25.5cm)

FINISHED SIZE

Length: approximately 13in (33cm)

Width: approximately 30in (76cm)

METHOD

1 Attach the 69 lengths of natural cord onto the lampshade frame using lark's head knots (see page 11).

The lampshade frame is divided into three sections. Each section will start with 23 lark's head knots and consist of three large 'V' patterns, and three smaller 'V' patterns, to which the tassels will be attached later.

2 Create the first 'V' pattern of double half hitch knots (see page 15) using 16 cords. Start on the left. The first cord will become the filler cord. Use the second cord to tie a double half hitch knot. Repeat with the next six cords.

3 Repeat Step 2 on the right, using cord 16 as the filler cord and working left towards the centre by tying seven more double half hitch knots.

4 The next 'V' pattern will begin using the 16th cord from the previous section as the first cord, which will be the filler cord. Tie seven diagonal double half hitch knots (see page 18) to the left and repeat on the right.

5 Repeat Step 4.

6 Repeat Steps 2–5 for the other two sections on the lampshade frame. This will complete the large 'V' pattern.

7 To make the smaller 'V' pattern, use the ten cords that sit between the two previous larger 'V' patterns. Starting from the left, and using the first cord as the filler cord, tie four diagonal double half hitch knots to the right. Repeat on the right, using the tenth cord as the filler cord and tying five diagonal double half hitch knots to the left.

8 Now repeat this a further eight times around the lampshade frame to complete the smaller 'V' pattern.

9 Brush out all the lengths of cord to create a fringe (see page 25) and cut 13in (33cm) from the frame rim. This will be the length of the finished piece.

10 To make the tassels, start by splitting the beige cords into 18 groups, each comprising three cords.

11 Brush out each group of three beige cords, and combine them to make a thicker cord.

12 Use these cords to make rya knots (see page 19) around the two central cords of each 'V' shape.

13 Brush the cord again and cut to 3½in (9cm) long.

14 Repeat Steps 11–13 a further 17 times.

Tip

For a fresh take on this contemporary piece, change both cords for contrasting colours to make a bright two-tone piece to match the colour scheme of your home.

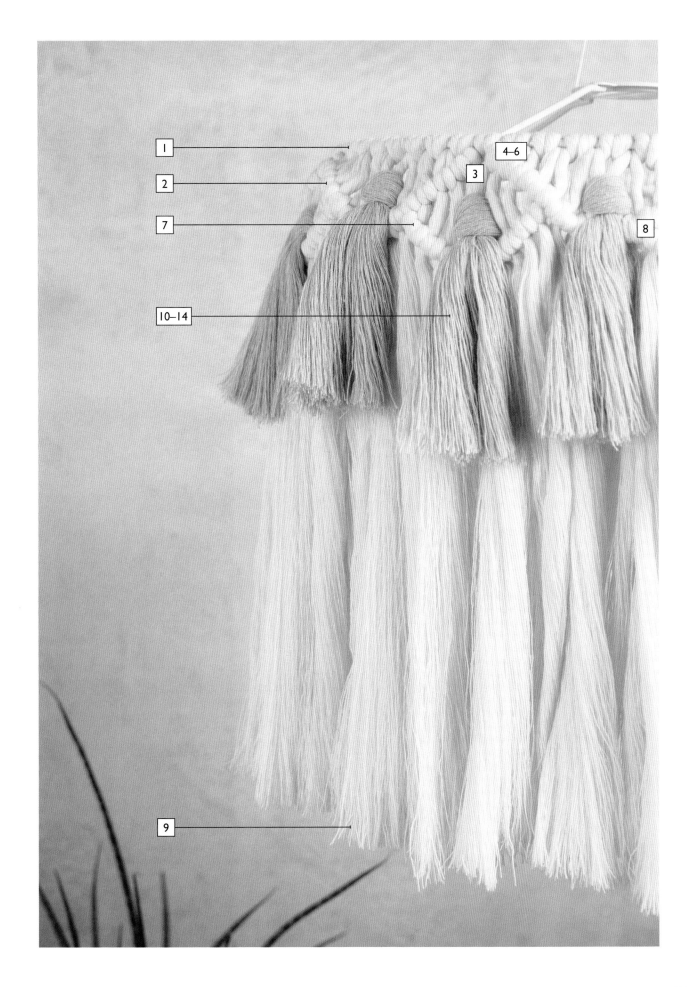

BOHO WALL HANGING

DESIGNED BY ISABELLA STRAMBIO

Full of natural shades and textures, this decorative wall hanging uses found objects to bring a unique and personal touch to the home. A contrasting copper ring adds polish to this earthy ensemble.

SKILL LEVEL: REQUIRES EXPERIENCE

YOU'LL NEED

- 4in (10cm) diameter copper hoop (or similar)

- 4 x 8–9in (20–23cm) long driftwood or wooden sticks

- 63yd (58m) of ¼in (5mm) single twist cotton cord in natural

- Tape measure

- Sharp scissors

- Tapestry needle

- Masking tape

KNOTS AND TECHNIQUES

- Lark's head knot

- Double half hitch knot

- Square knot

- Barrel knot

PREPARATION

Cut the following lengths of cord:

8 x 6¾yd (5.8m)

2 x 47in (1.2m)

1 x 31½in (80cm)

1 x 23½in (60cm)

4 x 71in (1.8m)

FINISHED SIZE

Length: approximately 55in (140cm)

Width: 9in (23cm)

METHOD

1 Tie the 6¾yd (5.8m) cords onto the copper hoop using lark's head knots (see page 11).

2 Fix the hoop to a flat surface with masking tape.

3 Leaving a gap of approximately 4in (10cm), take the first piece of driftwood and tie all the cords onto it using double half hitch knots (see page 15).

4 Repeat Step 3 with the second and third pieces of driftwood, keeping them as close as possible.

5 Separate the cords into four groups of four cords. Tie a sinnet of five square knots (see page 13) in each group.

6 Use a 47in (119cm) cord as a guide cord and tie five horizontal lines of double half hitch knots. Work from left to right. Tape one end of the guide cord to the left of your macramé on the flat surface to help you start. Don't worry about the ends of the guide cord – you can tape them at the back of the macramé with masking tape.

7 Take a 31½in (80cm) cord, turn your macramé over so the wrong side is facing and repeat Step 6, making three horizontal lines of double half hitch knots. Turn the macramé back around.

8 Take a 23½in (60cm) cord and repeat Step 6, making two horizontal lines of double half hitch knots.

9 Take the last piece of driftwood and tie the eight middle cords onto the driftwood using double half hitch knots. Place the unused cords at the back of the driftwood.

10 Use the second 47in (1.2m) cord as a guide cord and tie one horizontal line of double half hitch knots, working from right to left.

11 Take the eight cords in the middle and separate them into two groups of four. Tie a sinnet of three square knots with each group.

12 Take your guide cord from Step 10 and tie four horizontal lines of double half hitch knots using only the four cords on the left and right to tie the knots. Keep your guide cords behind the sinnets.

13 Use a 71in (1.8m) cord as a guide cord to tie one horizontal line of double half hitch knots, making sure that each end of your guide cord is approximately 31½in (80cm) long.

14 Use a 71in (1.8m) cord as a guide cord to tie one horizontal line of double half hitch knots, using just the 12 cords in the middle. Make sure that each end of your guide cord is approximately 31½in (80cm) long.

15 Use a 71in (1.8m) cord as a guide cord to tie one horizontal line of double half hitch knots, using just the eight cords in the middle. Make sure that each end of your guide is approximately 33½in (85cm) long.

16 Take a 71in (1.8m) cord and use as a guide cord to tie one horizontal line of double half hitch knots, using just the four cords in the middle. Make sure that each end of your guide cord is approximately 33½in (85cm) long.

17 Tie one or two barrel knots (see page 20) on each cord.

18 Trim the fringe to the desired length.

19 Turn your macramé over and trim the guide cords from Steps 6–12 to about 2in (5cm) and, with the help of a tapestry needle, tuck them behind one or two knots.

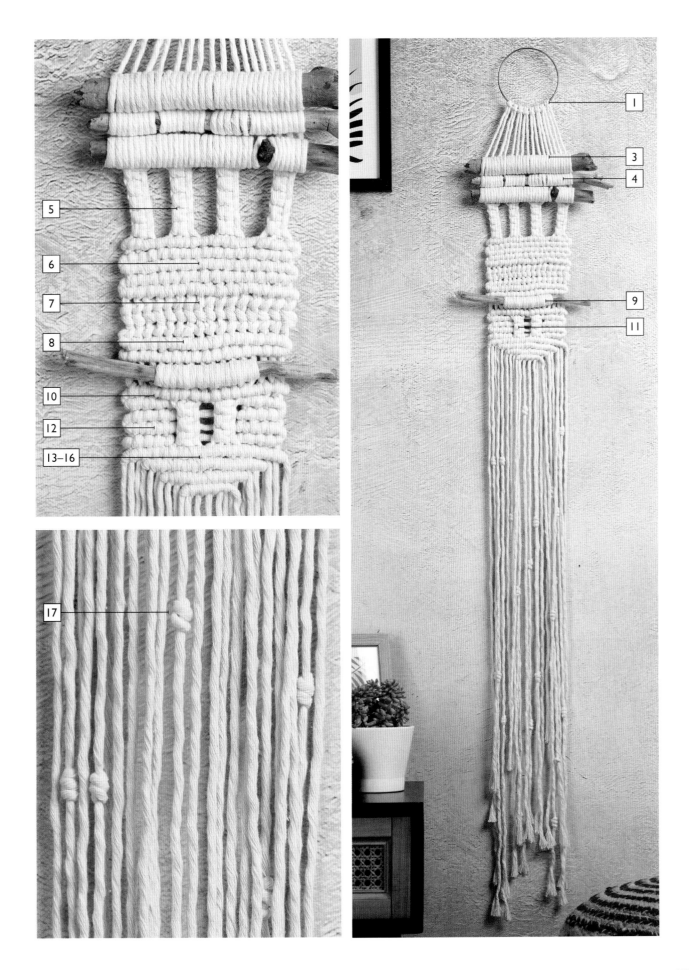

TABLE RUNNER

DESIGNED BY HANNAH McVIE

Learn the basic macramé knotting techniques with this impressive table runner. Once complete, use it to add effortless boho chic to a large coffee, dining or garden table.

SKILL LEVEL: EASY

YOU'LL NEED

- Adjustable clothes rail or wooden dowel rod to attach cords to while you work

- 96yd (88m) of ¼in (5mm) braided cotton cord in natural

- Tape measure

- Sharp scissors

- Tapestry needle

KNOTS AND TECHNIQUES

- Lark's head knot

- Horizontal double half hitch knot

- Diagonal double half hitch knot

- Square knot

- Diagonal double half hitch knot

PREPARATION

Cut the following lengths of cord:

18 × 5yd (4.8m)

2 × 16in (41cm)

FINISHED SIZE

Length: approximately 45¾in (116cm)

Width: approximately 11in (28cm)

METHOD

1 Attach the 5yd (4.8m) lengths of cord onto the rail, using lark's head knots (see page 11).

2 Using one 16in (41cm) length of cord as your filler cord, create a row of horizontal double half hitch knots (see page 19), directly under the lark's head knots. Ensure this row is as straight as possible, as all of the measurements will be made according to this line. Leave a surplus amount of filler cord (approximately 2in [5cm]) at either end – you will neaten this up when finished.

3 Number your cords 1–36. In the centre, drop down 2in (5cm) and tie a square knot (see page 13) with cords 17–20. This will be the peak of your 'ʌ' pattern.

4 Working from the centre out to the left, complete this section by taking two cords from the previous knot and adding in another two from the side of it, creating a diagonal row of square knots. Use cords 17 and 18 from the first square knot and add in cords 15 and 16 to tie another square knot.

5 Continue tying square knots using the following bundles for each: 13–16, 11–14, 9–12, 7–10, 5–8, 3–6 and finally 1–4.

6 Now repeat this on the right, using cords 19–22, 21–24, 23–26, 25–28, 27–30, 29–32, 31–34 and 33–36.

7 In the centre, drop down 2in (5cm) and tie another square knot using cords 17–20. This will form the peak of a shorter 'ʌ' pattern of square knots.

8 Working from the centre out to the left, use cords 15–18, 13–16, 11–14 and 9–12 to tie square knots.

9 Now repeat this on the right, using cords 19–22, 21–24, 23–26 and 25–28.

10 Now make a 'ʌ' pattern, using diagonal double half hitch knots (see page 18). Using cord 18 as your filler cord, drop down 2in (5cm) to create your first row of diagonal double half hitch knots, working from the centre out to the right. Try to tie these knots so they are at a similar angle to the square knots above and continue until you reach the far right.

11 Repeat this on the left, using cord 19 as the filler cord.

12 In the centre, drop down 2¾in (7.5cm) and tie a square knot using cords 17–20. This will create the peak for the pyramid of square knots.

13 On the next row, tie two square knots made from bundles 15–18 and 19–22.

14 On the next row, tie three square knots made from bundles 13–16, 17–20 and 21–24.

15 On the next row, tie four square knots made from bundles 11–14, 15–18, 19–22 and 21–24.

16 On the last row, tie five square knots made from bundles 9–12, 13–16, 17–20, 21–24 and 25–28.

17 In the centre, drop down 2in (5cm) and repeat Steps 3–6.

18 Create a 'ʌ' pattern directly beneath using diagonal double half hitch knots. Repeat Steps 10 and 11.

19 In the centre, drop down 2in (5cm) and tie a square knot using cords 17–20. This will create the peak for the diamond of square knots. Then repeat Steps 13–16.

20 Repeat Steps 15–12 to create the bottom of the diamond shape. This is the centre of the table runner.

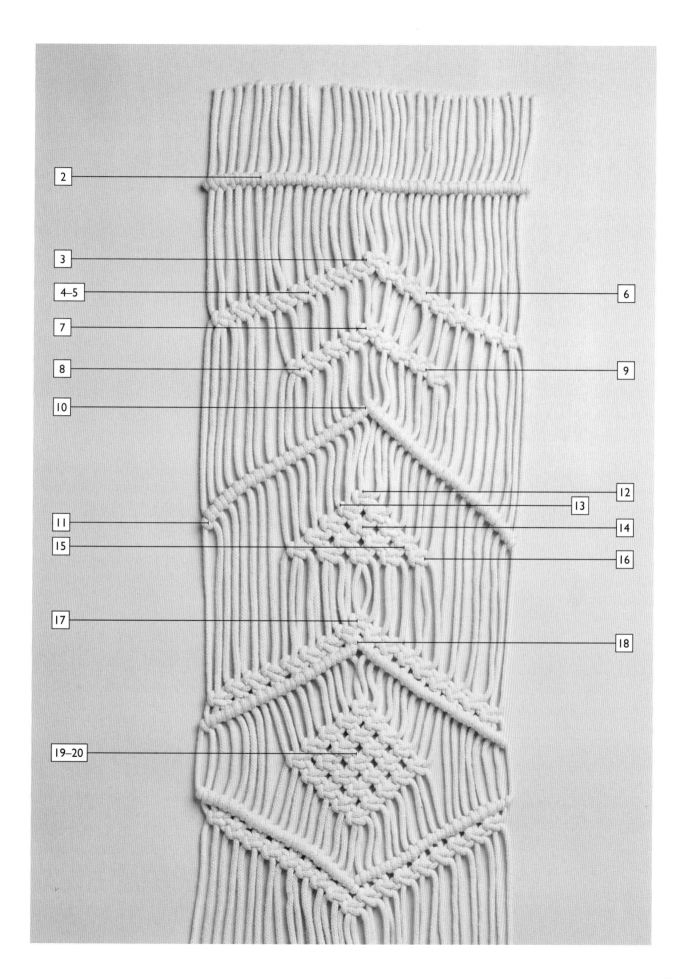

2

3

4–5

7

8

10

11

15

17

19–20

6

9

12

13

14

16

18

21 Now make a 'V' pattern using diagonal double half hitch knots. Using cord 1 as the filler cord, drop down 2in (5cm) from the last row of diagonal double half hitch knots to create your first row of diagonal double half hitch knots, working from left to right. Try to tie these knots so they are at a similar angle to the '⋏' of square knots above.

22 Repeat this from right to left using cord 36 as the filler cord.

23 Directly beneath, create a 'V' pattern using square knots. Working from left to right, use cords 1–4, 3–6, 5–8, 7–10, 9–12, 11–14 and 13–16 to create the square knots.

24 Working from right to left, use cords 33–36, 31–34, 29–32, 27–30, 25–28, 23–26, 21–24, 19–22 and 17–20 to create square knots.

25 In the centre, drop down 3in (7cm) and tie a square knot using cords 17–20. This will create the centre of the bottom row of the pyramid of square knots. Tie two square knots, using bundles 9–12 and 13–16. Then tie two more, using cords 21–24 and 25–28.

26 On the next row, tie four square knots made from bundles 11–14, 15–18, 19–22 and 21–24.

27 On the next row, tie three square knots made from bundles 13–16, 17–20 and 21–24.

28 On the next row, tie two square knots made from bundles 15–18 and 19–22.

29 On the last row, tie one square knot using cords 17–20 to form the bottom of the pyramid.

30 On the left, drop down 5½in (14cm) from the 'V' pattern of the square knots above. This is where you'll start your row of diagonal double half hitch knots using cord 1 as the filler cord, working from left to right until you reach cord 18.

31 Repeat on the right, using cord 36 as your filler cord. Once finished, there should be a gap of 2in (5cm) between this row and the previous square knot.

32 Drop down 2in (5cm) at cord 9 and tie your first square knot using cords 9–12. This is the start of a shorter 'V' pattern of square knots.

33 Continue working from left to right using bundles 11–14, 13–16 and 15-18.

34 Now repeat this on the right, using cords 25–28, 23–26, 21–24 and 19–22. Join these two sides together by forming another square knot using cords 17–20.

35 On the left, drop down 6½in (16.5cm) and tie a square knot with cords 1–4. This will be the start of the last 'V' pattern of square knots.

36 Working from right to left, complete this section by tying square knots using bundles 3–6, 5–8, 7–10, 9–12, 11–14 and 13–16, working towards the centre.

37 Repeat this on the right, using cords 33–36, 31–34, 29–32, 27–30, 25–28, 23–26, 21–24, 19–22 and 17–20 to tie square knots.

38 Using the other 16in (41cm) length of cord as your filler cord, drop down 4in (10cm) on the left and create a row of horizontal double half hitch knots as the last row of your table runner. In the centre there should be a gap of around 2¼in (5.5cm) between the square knot and the row of half hitches.

39 Once complete and no further adjustments are required, your table runner can now be cut from the rail. Turn your project so that the wrong side is facing towards you and cut the centre loop of each of the lark's head knots you tied at the beginning.

40 Tidy up the filler cords by weaving the cords from your rows of horizontal double half hitch knots (at either end of your table runner) through the back of those rows. I thread mine around four or five times and then trim them for a neat finish.

41 Finally, trim the fringe at either end of the finished piece to 3in (7cm).

Tip

For an alternative to this timeless classic, increase the number of cords and their lengths to make a bed runner or a longer table runner.

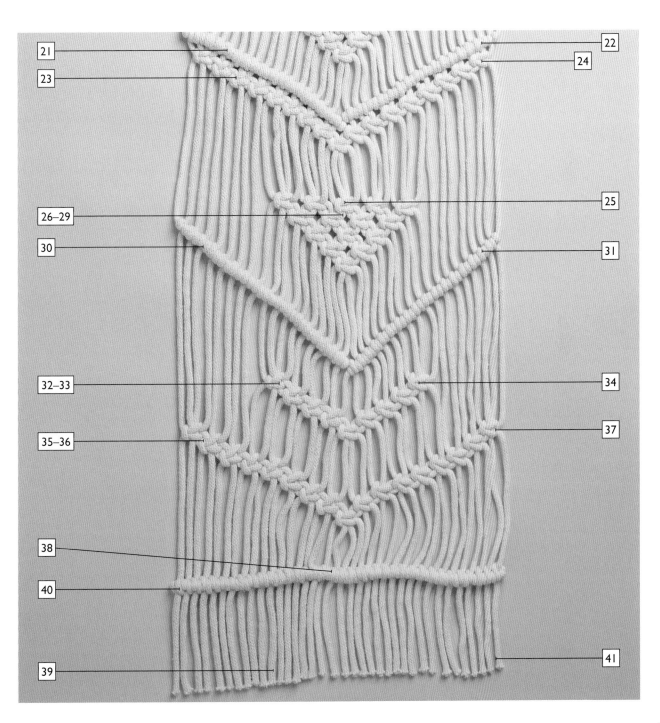

RETRO DOUBLE HANGER

DESIGNED BY EVE WINTER

This double plant hanger, inspired by retro styles, is a lovely way to display attractive houseplants. Bringing together a few different macramé techniques, this piece provides a great opportunity to try out different knotting combinations.

SKILL LEVEL: REQUIRES EXPERIENCE

YOU'LL NEED

- 3in (7cm) diameter wooden ring

- 57¼in (52.5m) of ¼in (5mm) 3-ply cord in orange

- 2 x 7in (18cm) lengths of scrap cord

- 8 x ¾in (20mm) wooden beads with ¼–½in (6–10mm) holes

- Tape measure

- Sharp scissors

- Tapestry needle or crochet hook

- Masking tape

KNOTS AND TECHNIQUES

- Overhand knot

- Turk's head knot

- Square knot

- Half knot

- Switch knot

- Berry knot

- Fraying

PREPARATION

Cut the following lengths of cord (see Tip, page 64):

4 x 4yd (4m)

4 x 8yd (7.7m)

3 x 59in (1.5m)

Pair together a 8yd (7.7m) and a 4yd (4m) cord. Feed them through the wooden ring, fold them in the middle and bundle them together with a loose overhand knot (see page 12). Repeat this with the remaining three pairs of cords.

FINISHED SIZE

Length: approximately 4¾ft (1.5m)

Small pot size: approximately 4¼in (11cm) in diameter

Large pot size: approximately 5¾in (14.5cm) in diameter

METHOD

1 Use one of the 59in (1.5m) cords to tie a Turk's head knot (see page 23) under the wooden ring, gathering all the cords together. Use a crochet hook or tapestry needle to feed the ends through the back of the knot, and neatly cut the excess cord.

2 Untie one set of cords and start by tying six square knots (see page 13), approximately 3in (7cm) in length.

3 Tie six left-facing half knots (see page 13) to create a spiral. Thread a bead onto the two filler cords and tie six right-facing half knots to create a spiral in the opposite direction.

4 Tie six more square knots underneath the spiral pattern that you have just created.

5 Tie a switch knot (see page 14) leaving a 1¼in (3cm) gap between each square knot. Repeat twice for a row of three switch knots. Repeat Steps 2–5 for the other three sets of cord.

6 Leave a 3in (7cm) gap and tie four alternating square knots to create the net for your plant hanger. Turn these square knots into berry knots (see page 16), and secure each berry knot with another square knot.

Take a scrap piece of cord and knot it tightly 3½in (9cm) below the berry knots, using an overhand knot (see page 12). Add your plant pot and adjust until you are happy with the placement. Cut the excess scrap cord and, using one of the 59in (1.5m) cords, tie a Turk's head knot around the scrap cord as you did in Step 1.

7 To begin the second part of the hanger, tie eight square knots, around 4in (10cm) in length. Create another spiral pattern from Step 3, and tie eight more square knots underneath.

8 Create another row of three switch knots. This time, leave a 1½in (4cm) gap between each one. Repeat Steps 8 and 9 for the remaining three sets of cords.

9 Repeat Steps 6 and 7 to complete the second net and the final Turk's head knot.

10 Trim the fringe so that the cords are the same length and gently unravel them, leaving a beautiful wavy texture. Don't brush this cord out, or you will lose the texture.

Tip

Three-ply cord unravels fairly easily. When you measure and cut each piece, mark it with masking tape before you cut through it. Cutting through the centre of the tape ensures that each piece of cord is protected, preventing it from unravelling, while also making it easier to work with.

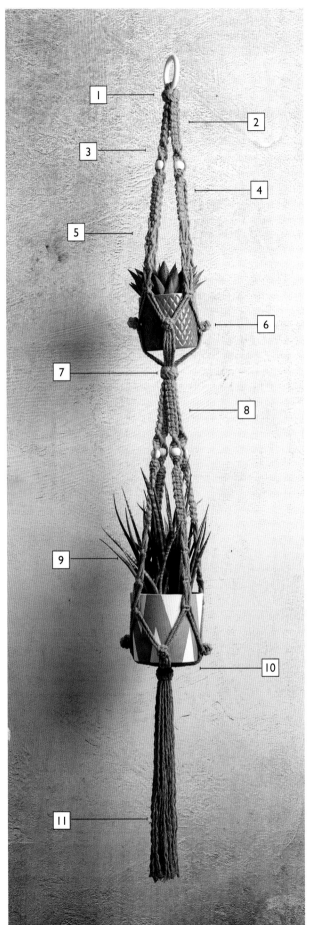

MINI WALL HANGING

DESIGNED BY LISA MILLER

Fantastic for beginners, this quick and easy mini macramé design will brighten up any wall. Make several in different colours and hang them in a row to create an interesting talking point in your home.

SKILL LEVEL: EASY

YOU'LL NEED

- 6in (15½cm) long wooden dowel rod

- 8½yd (7.8m) of ⅛in (3mm) cord in natural, pink or grey

- Tape measure

- Sharp scissors

- Comb

KNOTS AND TECHNIQUES

- Lark's head knot

- Double half hitch knot

- Reverse lark's head knot

- Fraying

- Brushing

PREPARATION

Cut the following lengths of cord:

6 x 30in (76cm)

2 x 15in (38cm)

11 x 9in (23cm)

FINISHED SIZE

Length: approximately 5in (12cm)

METHOD

1 Begin by attaching two 30in (76cm) lengths of cord to the middle of the dowel rod using a lark's head knot (see page 11).

2 Starting with the second cord from the left (working cord), tie a double half hitch knot (see page 15) across the remaining two pieces of cord. Finish by tying a lark's head knot onto the dowel rod with your working cord.

3 Then, attach another 30in (76cm) length of cord to the dowel rod using a lark's head knot, this time to the right side of your project.

4 Starting with the second cord on the right (working cord), tie a double half hitch knot across the remaining four pieces of cord. Again, finish by making a lark's head knot to tie the working cord to the dowel rod.

5 Attach another 30in (76cm) length of cord to the left side of your project using a lark's head knot. Take the second cord from the left (working cord) and tie a double half hitch knot across the next three cords.

6 Then, attach a 15in (38cm) cord to your working cord using a reverse lark's head knot (see page 11), and continue with the double half hitch knots across the remaining cords. Again, finish by tying the working cord to the dowel rod using a lark's head knot.

7 Attach another 30in (76cm) piece of cord to the right of your dowel rod using a lark's head knot. Use the second cord from the right as your working cord and tie the remaining pieces of cord using a double half hitch knot. Finish by attaching the working cord to the left of the dowel rod with a lark's head knot.

8 Leaving 1in (2cm) either side, attach your final 30in (76in) piece of cord to the dowel rod using a lark's head knot. Then attach the 11 pieces of 9in (23cm) cord to this with a reverse lark's head knot.

9 Finally, comb out the cord (see page 25) and trim it to your desired length. You can leave your macramé like this, or you can attach the remaining length of cord to your dowel rod so you can hang the piece more easily, as I have here.

1–2

5–6

7

3–4

8

9

BOHO WREATH

DESIGNED BY TABITHA MORGAN-EARP

Upcycle an embroidery hoop to create a stunning geometric macramé wreath. Once you start this simple piece, which uses just two types of knots, you won't believe how quickly it will grow! Experiment with using different coloured macramé cords or try using two different shades for a varied effect.

SKILL LEVEL: EASY

YOU'LL NEED

- 8in (20cm) wooden embroidery hoop

- 8½yd (35m) of ¼in (4–5mm) single twist cord in burgundy

- Ribbon, cord or string for hanging

- Tape measure

- Sharp scissors

- Comb

- Hairspray or spray-on starch

KNOTS AND TECHNIQUES

- Lark's head knot

- Half hitch knot

- Fraying

- Brushing

PREPARATION

Cut the following length of cord:

56 × 23½in (60cm)

FINISHED SIZE

Length: approximately 15½in (40cm)

Width: approximately 15½in (40cm)

METHOD

1 Fold each cord in half and attach it with a lark's head knot (see page 11) around the hoop until it's completely covered. If you prefer, you can also work by attaching the cords in sections so you don't have lots of loose cords.

2 Begin at the top of the embroidery hoop (where the tension screw is). Turn the hoop so the tension screw is at the bottom and start working with the cords next to it. Gather 12 cords on the hoop – this will be your first triangle.

3 To start the first row of the triangle, take cords 5 and 6 of your section and tie a half hitch knot (see page 15) diagonally inwards on cord 5 (two knots).

4 Working now from the right side, take cords 7 and 8 and repeat Step 3. With the two cords that meet, complete one final half hitch knot, ensuring you place the right over left to join this first line of the triangle. You should have six complete half hitch knots in this triangle.

5 For the next row of the triangle, repeat all the steps above, but begin with cords 3 and 4 for the left side and 10 and 11 for the right. In the second triangle you should have a total of 14 knots.

6 For the third row of the triangle you should now be left with cords 1 and 2 on the left, and 11 and 12 on the right. Work these in the same way and complete your final rows of half hitch knots either side of your triangle. In the third row you should now have a total of 22 knots.

7 The next triangle is smaller so you will need to gather eight cords. Work only two rows to complete this triangle using half hitch knots.

8 In the first row of your smaller triangle you should have six knots in total; in the second row you should have 14 knots.

9 In between the two completed triangles you can now create a two-row triangle. Using the six central cords left over from both adjacent triangles, make a two-row half hitch knot triangle.

10 Working alternately, repeat this pattern all the way around your hoop. The next triangle will be a larger one, followed by a smaller one and so on. Don't forget to add your smaller two-row triangles in between every triangle. The last triangle to meet with the tension screw should be a large triangle to match the first one you created. The completed triangles can move from side to side if you have left too much or too little space when creating the wreath.

Trimming:

Once you've finished working around the hoop you will have different lengths of cord left over. Place the hoop on a flat surface and ensure all the cords are lying flat with none tucked underneath. Using sharp scissors, cut the cords to around 2in (5cm) long, following the line of the triangles you've created. You can use some card or a finger width to measure as you go.

Once cut, you can now brush or comb the tassels (see page 25). Hold your work firmly and start to brush. The tassels will begin to untwist and become flat, but keep brushing and flattening them with your hand. Once brushed, the cords will be longer so you may need to re-trim the piece, again using some card or a finger width as a guide. For extra hold, and to ensure your tassels stay up once they're hung, you can use some hairspray or spray-on starch to spritz the tassels, gently patting them with your hands as you go. Spray both sides of the piece and leave it to dry.

Finally, use a piece of cord, ribbon or string to hang the hoop. Tie the loop around the tension screw at your desired length.

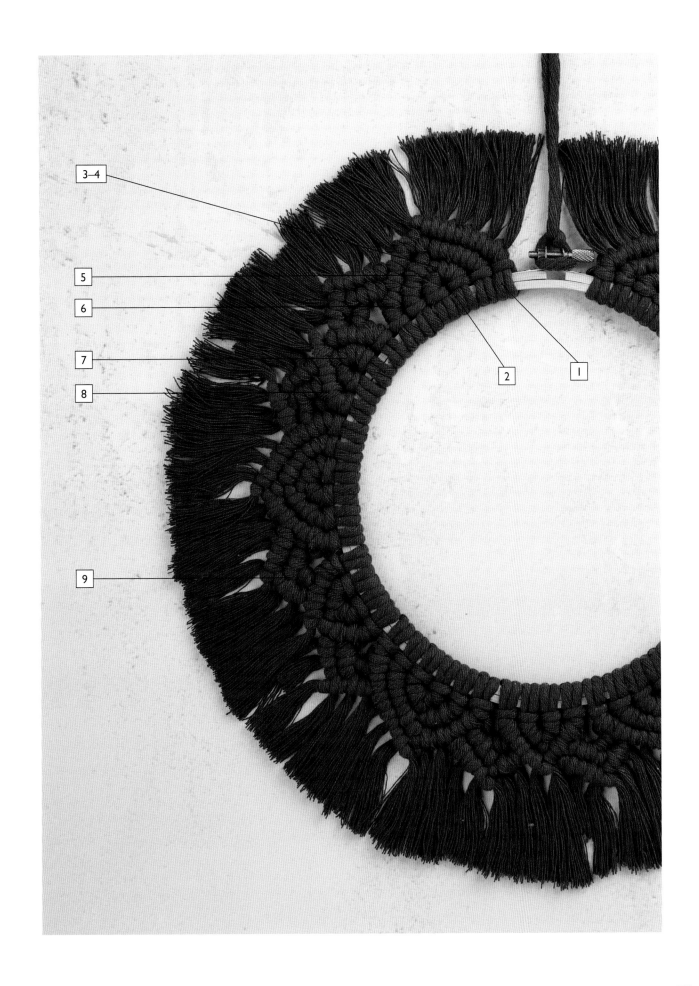

LIVING WALL

DESIGNED BY SARAH LAVINAY

Bring nature inside with a macramé 'living wall'. This unusual design is easy to make and will provide an interesting new home for your indoor plants.

SKILL LEVEL: EASY

YOU'LL NEED

- 27 x 39in (68.5cm x 1m) black grid mesh panel

- 295yd (270m) of ⅛in (3mm) single twist cotton cord in natural

- Tape measure

- Sharp scissors

- Comb

- Hairspray or spray-on starch

KNOTS AND TECHNIQUES

- Square knot

- Lark's head knot

- Wrap knot

- Feather knot

- Fraying

- Brushing

PREPARATION

Cut the following lengths of cord:

PLANT HOLDER
20 x 8ft (2.5m)
This will make one small plant holder (repeat four times).

26 x 8ft (2.5m)
This will make one large plant holder.

5 x 39in (1m)

FEATHERS
8 x 12in (30.5cm) and 1 x 19½in (50cm)
This will make one big feather (repeat five times).

8 x 8in (20cm) and 1 x 16in (41cm)
This will make one medium feather (repeat eight times).

5 x 7in (18cm) and 1 x 12in (30.5cm)
This will make one small feather (repeat six times).

FINISHED SIZE

Height: 27in (68.5cm)

Width: 39in (1m)

Small pot size: approximately 3¾in (9.5cm) in diameter

Large pot size: approximately 5¾in (14.5cm) in diameter

METHOD

PLANT HOLDER

1 Take one of the 8ft (2.5m) cords, fold it in half and secure it with a lark's head knot (see page 11) in the top first square from the left.

2 Take another 8ft (2.5m) cord and fold it in half and secure it with a lark's head knot in the top second square from the left. Take another eight cords and fix them the same way in the second top square.

3 Take nine more cords and fix those the same way in the third top square from the left. Add one more cord on the fourth top square from the left.

4 Tie a row of ten square knots (see page 13).

5 Leaving out the two cords at the beginning and end, make a row of nine alternating square knots.

6 Continue making rows of alternating square knots, dropping two cords at the beginning and end of every row until you have formed a triangle shape.

7 Take the middle four cords of the triangle shape and start another square knot, leaving approximately 2½–3in (7–8cm) between the end of the triangle and your new square knot.

8 Form another triangle with square knots using 20 cords, leaving ten cords on either side untouched.

9 Once the triangle is complete, take the two outside cords on either side to form a square knot. This will form the front part of the plant holder.

10 Move the two outside cords to the inside of your square knot.

11 Once you have formed the first square knot, take another two cords from the left and form a

square knot using those cords and two outside cords from the square knot above.

12 Continue this process, moving to the left until you have no outside cords left.

13 Repeat the same on the right side to make square knots going to the right.

14 Take the four middle cords of the open triangle shape and form a large square knot using the two outside cords on each side as working cords and the middle four as filler cords.

15 To close the diamond shape, start on the left and take the first two cords from the left row of square knots you have made, and two cords from the large, middle square knot that you made in Step 8. Form another square knot. Repeat the process until you've reached the middle of the diamond shape. Then, follow the same steps on the right side until you have closed the diamond shape.

16 You now have a back and a front layer that will need to be joined together to hold your plant pot. Use a square knot to close off the sides.

17 Use the 39in (1m) cord to close the bottom of the plant holder with an overhand knot.

18 Take another 39in (1m) cord to cover the cotton cord with a 1¼in (3cm) wrap knot (see page 17) and trim the cords to around 6in (15cm) in length.

19 Now you have completed the first small plant holder. Repeat Steps 1–18 to complete the plant holder on the top right.

20 For the second layer of plant holders, follow the same process, but use 26 cords instead of 20 for he large plant holder in the middle (see page 74).

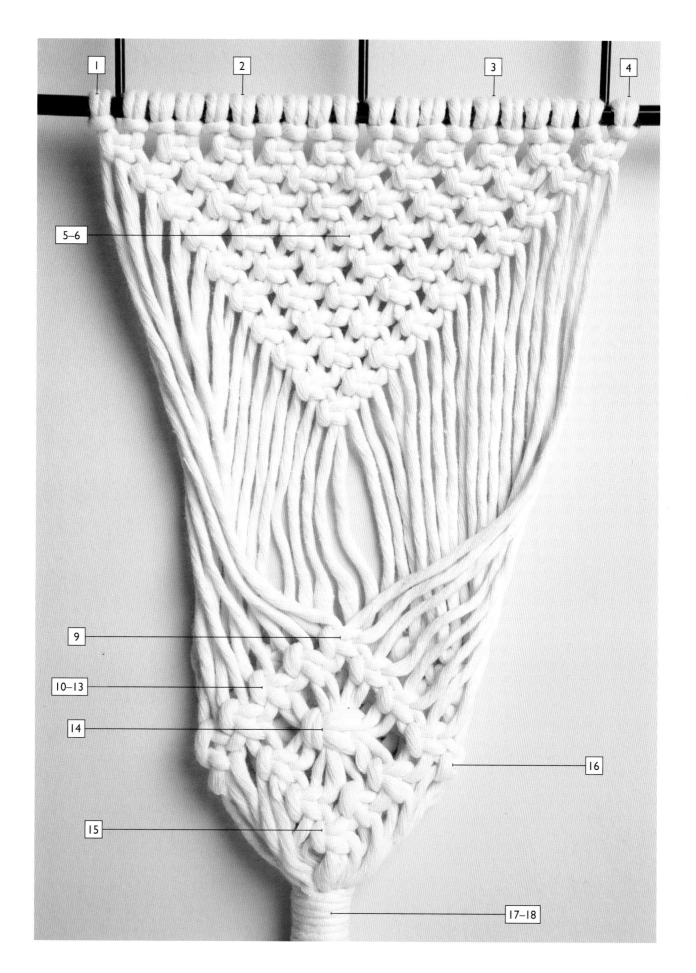

FEATHERS

The Living Wall has 19 feathers of different sizes. I always prepare three different sized templates to ensure each feather has the same shape. Use the feather knot instructions (see page 22) to make your feathers. Brush out the cords of each feather and cut to shape (see page 25).

Spray the brushed and pre-cut feathers with hairspray or spray-on starch and allow to dry before the final cut. Secure the feather in the metal mesh panel with leftover cord.

LARGE WALL HANGING

DESIGNED BY TABITHA MORGAN-EARP

This larger-than-life textural wall hanging is dramatic and bold. Ideal for someone ready to take their macramé skills to the next level, it is composed of several independent knotted panels, gradually brought together to create a stunning end result.

SKILL LEVEL: REQUIRES EXPERIENCE

YOU'LL NEED

- Adjustable clothes rail or fixed coat hook to hang piece from while you work

- 39–59in (1–1.5m) long wooden stick, stripped of bark and lightly sanded

- 148¾yd (136m) of ¼in (4.5–5mm) single twist cord in natural

- Tape measure

- Sharp scissors

- Comb

KNOTS AND TECHNIQUES

- Lark's head knot

- Half hitch knot

- Square knot

- Half knot

- Diagonal double half hitch knot

- Fraying

- Brushing

PREPARATION

Cut a 59in (1.5m) length of cord to hang up the piece while you're working. Use a length of scrap to start off if you're unsure where to place the final hanging cord.

Cut the following lengths of cord:

Central section
6 × 6½ft (2m)
26 × 5¾ft (1.8m)

Spiral knot section
4 × 10ft (3m)

Diamond half hitch knot section
8 × 10ft (3m)

Final tassel section
2 × 39in (1m)
75 × 19in (48cm)

FINISHED SIZE

Length: approximately 39in (1m)

Width: approximately 47in (1.2m)

METHOD

Central Section:

1 Start by attaching the 59in (1.5m) length of cord to the wooden stick, using a larks head knot (see page 11). Tie the cord securely so you can work at a good tension. It's best to hang the cord on more than one hook, for example a coat hook strip with four hooks. It's important not to hang the work up too high, so your arms don't get too tired.

2 Attach the 6½ft (2m) lengths of cord to your stick. Start by placing two cords in the middle, side by side, using a lark's head knot. Then add the second set of two cords to the left, about 4–6in (10–15cm) away from your central cords, repeat on the right. Make a square knot (see page 13) under each pair to secure.

3 You should have 12 working cords. To begin, take the two inner cords from the left side and the two right cords from the middle section, make a square knot around 4in (10cm) down from the stick. This should create a triangle and leave the two cords on the left. Repeat this on the right side. You should now have two triangles. To finish this section, take two inner cords from each square knot you've just made and create a final square knot around 4in (10cm) down. You should now have two triangles and a diamond.

4 On the left side of your work you can now start to attach the 26 cords (cut at 5¾ft [1.8m] in length each and folded in half). Next to your two free cords, add seven cords in this first section with a lark's head knot, you should finish at a square knot (16 working cords). Make sure to do the lark's head knot over both cords, and don't worry if the line is not full, this helps with creating a flat half hitch knot (see page 15) later.

5 Then, add six cords to the lower left section until you reach the middle (14 working cords, including two cords from the central square knot). Repeat this step on the other side; add seven cords to the right upper side and six to the lower section.

6 Working from the left side again, you can now start a line of diagonal double half hitch knots (see page 18) all the way down, working towards the centre of the piece. Make sure to include the two leftover cords at the top. Repeat this on the right side. Try to keep the knots close to your lark's head knots, this will help you to create the slightly scalloped look.

7 To create the next row of half hitch knots, count 17 cords from the top of the work on the right. Start your next row of half hitch knots on cord 18. Work this line until you reach the middle, and using the two cords that meet (one from the left side), complete one final half hitch knot, making sure to wrap the left cord over the right. Repeat on the left side. This side should fit in nicely under the row you've just made.

8 To create the last row, count 21 cords from the top of your work on the left side and start a row of half hitch knots, working towards the centre. Repeat on the right, but this time when you get to the end of the row and you have reached the left-side cord, wrap the left cord over the right to create an overlapped look. The central section is now complete.

Spiral Knot Section:

1 Attach two 10ft (3m) length pieces (folded in half) about 4–6in (10–15cm) away from your last pair on the left. Repeat on the right.

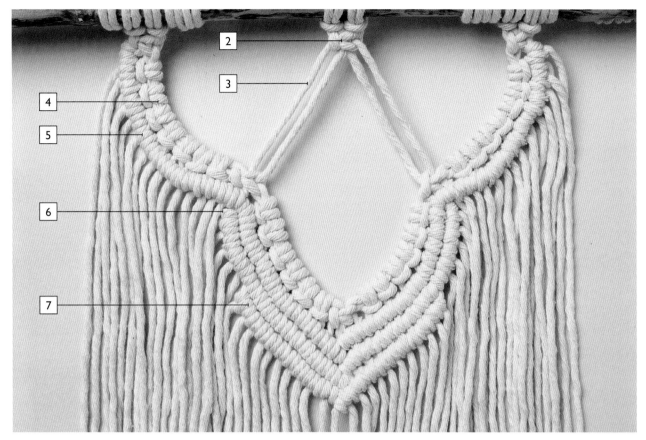

2 Work a half knot (see page 13) over and over to create a spiral. Work until the spirals measure around 6in (15cm). You will need to swap and use the central cords you have been spiralling around. Simply take the inner cords and work a half knot around the previous outer cords and pull them tight. This should disguise the swap over. Work until the spiral measures 12–14in (30–36cm).

3 Repeat this on the right side, making sure to swap to the central cords approximately 6in (15cm) down, otherwise you won't have enough to join in the middle. Make sure the two spirals meet under the central point that you created in the previous section.

4 To join the two spirals together, simply take the outer two cords from each spiral and join them with a square knot. You can continue with a spiral at this point but it will be chunkier and you will need to be careful that you don't run out of cord.

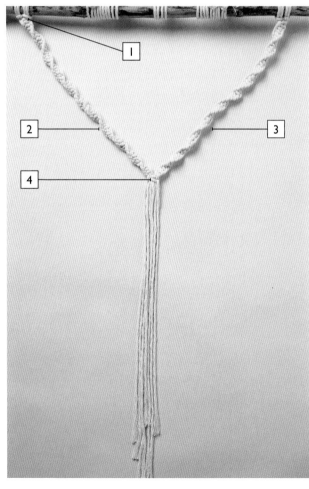

Diamond Half Hitch Knot Section:

1 Attach four 10ft (3m) cords (folded in half) to the right and left of your work, 4–6in (10–15cm) away from your spiral knot sections.

2 To begin, take the four inner cords. Using the left two cords only, work a diagonal double half hitch knot, taking the cords from the left (outwards) as you work diagonally down towards the left outer side of the piece. Then take the right two inner cords and work diagonally outwards with diagonal double half hitch knots. You should have six diagonal double half hitch knots on both sides in total.

3 Working on the left side, take the top inner cord and begin to work a diagonal double half hitch knot, but work the line inwards to create the diamond shape. Then, take the next cord down and repeat until you have 12 knots on the left side. By using the top cord and working down, you should create a 'turned over' look in the middle.

4 Working on the right side, repeat the process from Step 3 but in the opposite direction. You should now have a diamond shape.

5 Join the two long cords in the middle using a diagonal double half hitch knot, but make sure to wrap the left cord around the right one. This starts off your second diamond and creates an overlay or twisted effect.

6 Continuing with this longer cord, work the left side cords following the line diagonally down to create one long line. Stop when you have used the three cords on the left.

7 Work the right side as in Step 6, but in the opposite direction. It should look as though it's coming from underneath the longer line and as if your diamonds are twisted together.

8 Repeat Steps 2–7 to create eight more diamonds in the left section. Your central cords will be longer, leave them for now and you can trim them at the end.

9 Repeat Steps 2–7 on the right side to create a matching diamond section.

Final Tassel Section:

1 Start by attaching the 39in (1m) cord 4–6in (10–15cm) away from the left diamond section. Use a lark's head knot to attach the cord.

2 Unhook and turn your piece over, so you're working on the back. Then, taking the cord inwards and leaving around a 6in (10cm) drop in the middle of the cord, attach the ends between the two right central sections. To attach, wrap each end over twice and tie to secure, making sure to cross around the front of the cord. Don't worry if there is length leftover as this will become a tassel.

3 You can now unhook and turn your work back around. Start to add your 19in (48cm) lengths and using lark's head knots, add 36 to the right side. The knots can be evenly spaced afterwards. If you prefer, you could also add longer lengths of cord at this point.

4 Repeat Steps 1–3 on the left side. Your piece is now ready to trim and comb.

Trimming:

Lightly comb the ends of the shorter tassels, 2–4in (5–10cm) from the bottom. If you prefer a neat look, trim the tassels using a pair of sharp scissors.

Either cut the longer central tassels freehand or, working your way from the outside in, take a few cords from each side and bring them together in the middle and cut them to your desired length.

You can also comb the ends of these tassels and re-trim the cords if you want a perfect straight edge.

NECKLACE

DESIGNED BY FALLON KNOWLES

This elegant necklace will add contemporary style to any outfit. Made using chunky braided cotton cord, the pretty plaited effect is created by repeating identical knots over and over. Simple jewellery fittings add a stylish finishing touch.

SKILL LEVEL: REQUIRES EXPERIENCE

YOU'LL NEED

- 11ft (3.3m) of ¼in (5mm) braided cotton cord in blue

- 2 x ½ x ⅜in (8 x 12mm) end caps

- 2 x ¼in (5mm) jump rings

- 1 x lobster clasp

- Tape measure

- Sharp scissors

- Glue gun

- Pliers

- Cocktail stick

PREPARATION

Cut the following length of cord:

1 x 11ft (3.3m)

FINISHED SIZE

Length: (unfastened) 19in (48cm)

METHOD

1 Fold the cord in half so you're working with two cords together. Start from the end that is folded in half and create a loop 10in (25cm) down from the top of the cord. The longer piece of cord is now going to become the working cord.

2 Take the doubled working cord under the loop and through, to create a second loop inside about 2in (5cm) in size.

3 Repeat this again, taking the working cord behind the second loop and through, to create a new loop.

4 Continue to repeat Step 3, keeping an eye on the tension and keeping the loop the same size as you go. Repeat this ten times.

5 To finish the necklace, take the working cord and push it through the last loop you made and pull through to close the necklace. Turn the necklace over to see the final pattern. Trim all four cords so they are equal.

6 Put a small amount of glue into one of the end caps and insert the ends of the cord from one side of the necklace. Repeat for the other side. I use a cocktail stick to push the ends of the cord into the end cap.

7 Finally, attach the lobster clasp to one jump ring, and then each jump ring to an end cap.

Tip

If you want to make the necklace longer, you can increase the amount of cord you use and start further down the cords, or use a longer piece of cord and repeat Step 4.

HANGING BASKET

DESIGNED BY ISABELLA STRAMBIO

This versatile hanging basket is great for plants but can also be used to hold fruit, toys, toiletries and a lot more besides. Attractive and functional, the basket adds a touch of style and texture to your surroundings.

SKILL LEVEL: REQUIRES EXPERIENCE

YOU'LL NEED

- 1 x 3in (7cm) diameter wooden ring
- 2 x 8in (20cm) diameter wooden hoops
- 139yd (127m) of ¼in (5mm) 3-ply cotton cord in natural
- Tape measure
- Sharp scissors

KNOTS AND TECHNIQUES

- Lark's head knot
- Reverse lark's head knot
- Half knot
- Square knot
- Double half hitch knot
- Wrap knot
- Overhand knot

PREPARATION

Cut the following lengths of cord:

6 x 6½yd (6m)

36 x 8ft (2.5m)

1 x 3ft (1m)

FINISHED SIZE

Length: approximately 8in (20.5cm)

Width: approximately 4¾ft (1.5m)

METHOD

1 Tie the 6½yd (6m) cords onto the wooden ring using a lark's head knot (see page 11). The two cords in the middle should face the opposite side.

2 Leave a gap of approximately 8in (20cm). Start from the left, take the first four cords and tie a sinnet of 25 half knots (see page 13) approximately 5½in (14.5cm) long. Repeat with all the cords to make a total of three sinnets.

3 Leave a gap of approximately 8in (20cm). Tie three new sinnets of 20 half knots.

4 Take one of the wooden hoops and tie the cords onto it with a double half hitch knot (see page 15). For each set of cords, tie the two cords in the middle first and then the outer two. Make sure the three sets of cords are spaced out equally on the wooden hoop.

5 Tie the 36 8ft (2.5m) cords on the wooden hoop, 12 cords on each gap with a reverse lark's head knot (see page 11).

6 Take the four cords from one of the sinnets and two cords on the left and two on the right and tie a row of two square knots (see page 13).

7 Next, tie an alternating square knot with the four cords in the middle.

8 Repeat with the other two sets of sinnets.

9 Take the eight cords in the middle, between two sinnets, and make a row of two square knots and an alternating square knot underneath.

10 There are six unused cords left between the sets of square knots. Starting from the left, take the third string and use as a guide string. Tie a diagonal line of double half hitch knots using six cords and work from right to left. Repeat on the opposite side using the fourth cord as a guide cord.

11 Repeat with all the unused cords, making six half-diamond shapes.

12 Starting with one half-diamond, take the six cords in the middle and make a large square knot using two central cords as the filler cords and two cords on the left and two on the right as the working cords.

13 Next, close the diamond. Take the guide cords at each end and tie two lines of double half hitch knots. You have made the Type one diamond.

14 Take the next half-diamond and weave all the cords. Take the cords from the right diagonal and, one by one, weave them over and under the cords from the left diagonal. The first string will go under, then over and so on. The second string will go over, then under and so on. Continue with all the cords.

15 Next, close the diamond. Take the guide cords at each end and tie two lines of double half hitch knots. You have made the Type two diamond.

16 Alternate the Type one and two diamonds, working around the basket.

17 Make a Type two diamond under the Type one diamond and vice versa. Continue all around.

18 Between two of the bottom diamonds, tie a square knot and a row of two square knots underneath that repeat between all the diamonds.

19 Tie all the cords on the wooden hoop with double half hitch knots.

20 Group all the cords and tie a wrap knot (see page 17) using the 3ft (1m) string.

21 Trim the cords to the desired length and tie an overhand knot (see page 12) at the end.

TASSEL WALL HANGING

DESIGNED BY ABI WILLIAMS

These cute little wall hangings are just the thing for adding colour and interest to small spaces, door handles or as part of a gallery wall. The tassels can be customized to fit with your home decor, and for added variety, you could use ribbons, strips of patterned material or textured wool.

SKILL LEVEL: EASY

YOU'LL NEED

- 4in (10cm) long piece of dowel or wood

- 7yd (6.4m) of ⅛in (3mm) braided cotton cord in natural

- 19½yd (17.9m) of 1⁄16in (1.5mm) multi-coloured wool

- Tape measure

- Sharp scissors

KNOTS AND TECHNIQUES

- Lark's head knot

- Square knot

- Double half hitch knot

- Diagonal double half hitch knot

- Rya knot

- Overhand knot

PREPARATION

Cut the following lengths of cotton cord:

6 x 40in (1m)
1 x 15in (38.5cm)

Cut the following lengths of wool:
7 x 10in (25cm)

FINISHED SIZE

Length: approximately 7in (18cm)

Width: approximately 4in (10cm), depending on length of dowel used

METHOD

1 Attach the six lengths of 40in (1m) braided cord to the dowel using lark's head knots (see page 11).

2 Tie three square knots (see page 13) along the top row. For the second row, tie two square knots between the top row knots. For the third row, tie one square knot between the second row of knots to make an upside-down triangle shape.

3 Taking the top left cord, create a diagonal line down to the centre point of the triangle using diagonal double half hitch knots (see page 18). Then, do the same but starting from the top right cord, working down to the centre point of the triangle. Join the two rows in the middle using double half hitch knots. Repeat this step so you have created a double outline of the triangle.

4 Taking the first four cords on the left, tie a square knot. Repeat with the first four cords on the right. Below the square knot on the left, take the two right-hand cords and the two open cords to the right of these and tie a square knot. Repeat this on the right-hand side, using the two left cords and the two open cords to the left of these. Create a central square knot below these, using the middle four cords (the right-hand two from the left side and the left-hand two from the right). This should make a 'V' shape following the lines of the double half hitch knots from Step 3.

5 Taking the top left cord, create a diagonal line down to the centre point of the triangle using double half hitch knots. Then, do the same starting from the top right cord down to the centre point of the triangle. Repeat this step, but leave a small gap between the rows as this is where you will attach the tassels. You will now have a double outline of the triangle.

6 Using your 10in (25cm) long pieces of multi-coloured wool, separate into seven piles to give you ten lengths for each tassel. Beginning in the middle and using rya knots (see page 19), attach the tassels to the wall hanging. Working outwards to the edge, place your tassels between your last two rows of half hitch knots (the second row will be hidden behind the tassels).

7 Trim the tassels to the desired length and shape.

8 Using the cord for the handle, take the left-hand end and tie a double overhand knot (see page 12) around the left-hand end of the dowel. Repeat on the right. Adjust the knots so it hangs at the desired length, tuck the ends into the back of the lark's head knots and trim the ends.

Tip

If you're using something thicker than 1⁄16in (1.5mm) wool for the tassels, you will probably need to adjust the quantity of lengths per tassel. For example, if using 1⁄8in (3mm) single twist macramé cord, I would use only three pieces per tassel.

BAG

DESIGNED BY STEPH BOOTH

This stylish bag is an essential accessory to accompany you on your summertime adventures. Its cascading tassels and acrylic handles will help to add colour and texture to your look.

SKILL LEVEL: REQUIRES EXPERIENCE

YOU'LL NEED

- Adjustable clothes rail (or wooden dowel rod) and S-hooks to hang bag from while you work

- 2 x 5in (12cm) diameter acrylic handles

- 63yd (58m) of ⅛in (3mm) 3-ply cotton cord in green

- Tape measure

- Sharp scissors

KNOTS AND TECHNIQUES

- Lark's head knot

- Square knot

- Half knot

- Wrap knot

PREPARATION

Cut the following lengths of cord:

28 x 6½ft (2m)

8 x 10in (25cm)

FINISHED SIZE

Length: (including handles) approximately 16¾in (43cm)

Width: approximately 8¼in (21cm)

METHOD

1 Take one handle and attach it to an S-hook, then hang this from the clothes rail. Fold 14 of the 6½ft (2m) green cords in half and attach them to the first handle using lark's head knots (see page 11).

2 Starting on the left, take the first four cords and tie a row of seven square knots (see page 13).

3 Repeat Step 2.

4 Starting on the left with cords 3–6, tie a row of six square knots.

5 Repeat Step 4.

6 Repeat Steps 2 and 3.

7 Repeat Steps 1–6 for the second handle.

8 Bring both handles together so that the front of the design is facing outwards on both sides of the bag.

9 Join the sides of the bag together by tying a row of 14 square knots.

10 Repeat Step 9.

11 Starting on the left, tie a row of 14 left-facing half knots (see page 13) to create a spiral with eight left half knots in each twist.

12 Starting on the left, tie a row of 14 square knots and repeat for another six rows, alternating the knots.

13 Lay the bag flat and make sure the handles are aligned evenly.

14 Align the square knots on the front and back of the last row and then tie eight wrap knots (see page 17) using the eight cut pieces of 10in (25cm) green cord. Secure the knot by pulling gently on both ends of the cord. Trim any excess cord.

15 You have now created the bag tassels. Using sharp scissors cut the ends of the tassels to your desired length.

> *Tip*
>
> Using the fraying or brushing technique (see page 25), you can create your desired finish for the bag tassels.

1

2–3

4–5

6

8–10

11

12

14

CINNAMON STICK DECORATIONS

DESIGNED BY TABITHA MORGAN-EARP

Deck the halls with macramé! A beautifully simple and wonderfully smelling project, these three cute decorations are sure to get you in the festive spirit. Adorn your tree, hang them on the wall in a row, or slip them over door handles to add texture and aroma to your holiday decor.

SKILL LEVEL: EASY

YOU'LL NEED

- Clipboard to hang the decoration while you work

- 3 x cinnamon sticks, approximately 4–6in (10–12cm) long

- 13¼yd (12m) of ⅛–¼in (4–5mm) single twist cord in natural

- String, ribbon or cord for hanging

- Comb

- Tape measure

- Sharp scissors

- Hairspray or spray-on starch

KNOTS AND TECHNIQUES

- Lark's head knot

- Diagonal double half hitch knot

- Fraying

- Brushing

PREPARATION

Cut the following lengths of cord:

12 x 39in (1m)

Fold four strands of cord in half and attach to each cinnamon stick using a lark's head knot (see page 11). You should now have eight working cords in total on each stick. Hang your work up to help you create good tension.

FINISHED SIZE

Length: approximately 6in (15cm)

Width: approximately 4in (10cm)

METHOD

First decoration (double diamond):

1 Take the four inner cords, and using the left two cords only, work a half hitch knot (see page 15), taking the cords from the left (outwards) as you work diagonally down towards the left outer side of the piece. Then take the right two inner cords and work diagonally outwards with half hitch knots. You should have six half hitch knots in total on each side.

2 Working on the left side, take the top inner cord and begin working a half hitch knot, working the line inwards to create the diamond shape. Then, take the next cord down and repeat until you have 12 knots on the left side. By using the top cord and working down, you should create a 'turned over' look in the middle.

3 Working on the right side, repeat Steps 1 and 2 but in the opposite direction. You should now have a diamond shape.

4 Join the two long cords in the middle using a half hitch knot, making sure that you wrap the left cord around the right one. This starts off your second diamond and creates an overlay or twisted effect.

5 Continuing with this longer cord, work the left side cords following the line diagonally down to create one long line. Stop when you have used the three cords on the left.

6 Work the right side as in Step 5, but in the opposite direction. It should look as though it's coming from underneath the longer line.

7 Repeat Steps 2 and 3 to create the second diamond. It should now look as though your diamonds are threaded together.

Second decoration (one diamond):

1 Take the two left side cords and begin to make a half hitch knot (see page 15). Then, using three cords on that side, work diagonally towards the middle of the decoration. In total you should have six knots on the left side.

2 Repeat using the two right-hand side cords.

3 Join the upside-down triangle together with the two long cords in the middle. Make sure that you wrap the right cord around the left one as this will create the overlap effect.

4 Continue working in this way, downwards and diagonally to the opposite side of the piece, left to right, until you have used the three cords on the right side.

5 Working on the left, work outwards diagonally using the three cords. You should now have a cross shape.

6 Take the top inner cord on the left and begin to work a half hitch knot, working the diamond inwards. Continue with the next thread and repeat until you have 12 knots on the left side. Repeat the process on the right side but in the opposite direction. To finish the diamond, work a half hitch knot, taking the right-hand strand over the left one to create the overlap. You should now have a triangle at the top and a diamond.

7 To finish, continue to work the cord you have just knotted over with the three cords on the right, working down diagonally.

8 Repeat this on the left side, working diagonally outwards using the three remaining cords.

Third decoration (chevron):

1 Take the two left cords and begin to work a half hitch knot (see page 15). Using the next three cords, work diagonally down towards the middle of the decoration. Work six knots.

2 Repeat on the right side, working towards the middle of the decoration.

3 To join, take the longer two middle cords and work a half hitch knot, taking the left cord over the right.

4 Repeat Steps 1, 2 and 3 for a total of six rows.

Trimming:

1 Place your work on a flat surface, making sure all the cords are flat and not tucked under the piece. Cut the cords to your desired length with sharp scissors. You can be creative here and cut however you feel is best. There are a variety of cutting styles for inspiration.

2 Holding the decoration firmly, use a comb to brush out the tassels. You may need to re-trim the ends slightly after brushing for a neat finish.

3 Finally, you can lightly spritz the tassels with hairspray or spray-on starch, patting down as you go to keep everything in place.

Tips

These decorations don't have to be made just for the festive season – they could be used as favours for a party or a wedding. Alternatively, try attaching the cords to a key chain to create a cute keyring. Always pull your knots tight at the end if you try this.

FEATHER LAMPSHADE

DESIGNED BY SARAH LAVINAY

This stunning lampshade is cleverly composed of many pretty macramé feathers, combined to create a unique and eye-catching centrepiece.

SKILL LEVEL: REQUIRES EXPERIENCE

YOU'LL NEED

- 12in (30.5cm) diameter lampshade frame
- 12in (30.5cm) diameter metal hoop
- 10in (25cm) diameter metal hoop
- 244yd (224m) of ⅛in (3mm) single twist cotton cord in natural, pearl and coffee
- 10ft (3m) of transparent cord or fishing wire
- 12 × ½in (14mm) wooden beads
- Tape measure
- Sharp scissors
- Glue gun
- Small piece of scrap cardboard
- Piece of paper
- Pencil
- Tapestry needle or crochet hook
- Comb
- Hairspray or spray-on starch

KNOTS AND TECHNIQUES

- Feather knot
- Fraying
- Brushing

PREPARATION

Cut the following lengths of cord:

1 × 4yd (4m) in coffee

20 × 8in (20cm) and 1 × 15½in (40cm)
This will make one big feather. Repeat 30 times, making 12 in coffee, 10 in pearl and 8 in natural.

12 × 7in (18cm) and 1 × 12in (30.5cm)
This will make one small feather. Repeat 30 times, making 12 in coffee, 10 in pearl and 8 in natural.

Cut the following lengths of transparent cord:

8 × 14¾in (37.5cm)

FINISHED SIZE

Length: approximately 19½in (50cm)

Diameter: 12in (30.5cm)

METHOD

1 Take the lampshade frame and wrap the 4yd (4m) cord tightly around the metal hoop to cover the metal. Secure occasionally using a glue gun to ensure the cord cannot move. Once the lampshade frame is covered with the cord you can start preparing the feathers.

2 Take one of the 15½in (40cm) cords and fold it in half, folding it over the metal hoop.

3 Take one of the ½in (14mm) wooden beads and take the two ends of the folded 15½in (40cm) cord and pull the bead through the hole right to the top.

4 Make a large feather knot (see page 22) with ten rows of cord under the wooden bead.

5 Be sure to push the strands up to tighten them, taking the bottom of the middle strand with one hand and pushing up the strands with the other.

6 You now have the first feather knot fixed on your metal lampshade frame. Repeat the same process for the remaining 11 feathers.

7 Prepare the small feathers using the feather knot. These sit in between the large feathers.

8 You should have 24 feathers on your first layer (12 big feathers and 12 small feathers).

9 Take the 12in (30.5cm) diameter metal hoop. Wrap the pearl cord tightly around the hoop and fix it at intervals with the glue gun.

10 You need to secure 20 feathers on this hoop (alternate ten big feathers and ten small feathers). Follow Steps 3–9 to secure the feathers on the metal hoop (excluding the wooden beads).

11 For the last layer, take the 10in (25cm) diameter metal hoop, tightly wrap around the natural cord and fix with a glue gun at intervals. This layer will have 16 feathers (alternate eight big feathers and eight small feathers). When all the feathers are fixed on the hoops you can start brushing and cutting.

12 Take the first layer with 24 feathers and lay it on a large flat surface. Feather by feather, brush the cord until smooth and cut into a feather shape (see page 22). Draw the outlines of the large and small feathers onto paper, cut them out and use as templates to trim your feathers into shape. Repeat the brushing and cutting for all the feathers.

13 Now give the feathers their final shape. Hang the first layer at a workable height, brush each feather and spray it with hairspray or spray-on starch. Once this has dried, give it a final trim. I used a small piece of cardboard as a base against which to brush and spray each feather. Follow this process for each feather until you have finished them all.

14 To put all three layers together, secure the second layer on the first layer using four transparent cords. Create a loop with each of the four transparent cords around the first and second metal hoop, so that the second metal hoop hangs on four cords from the first metal hoop. Secure the third layer in the same way, so that it hangs on four cords from the second metal hoop.

HOOP WALL HANGING

DESIGNED BY FLISS THOMPSON-LEES

What better way to add some modern vibes to your surroundings than to create this fringed hoop wall hanging? Different coloured cords can be used and you could also add some dried flowers or eucalyptus leaves. The wall hanging can be made bigger or smaller, depending on the size of the hoop.

SKILL LEVEL: EASY

YOU'LL NEED

- 10in (25cm) diameter metal hoop in black or gold
- 12yd (11m) of ⅛in (3mm) rope cord in natural
- Tape measure
- Sharp scissors
- Comb

KNOTS AND TECHNIQUES

- Reverse lark's head knot
- Square knot
- Double half hitch knot
- Wrap knot
- Brushing
- Fraying

PREPARATION

Cut the following lengths of cord:

14 x 30in (76.5cm)

2 x 40in (102cm)

8 x 30in (76.5cm)

5 x 14in (35cm)

FINISHED SIZE

Length: approximately 24in (61cm)

METHOD

1 Fold 14 of the 30in (76.5cm) and two of the 40in (102cm) cords in half. With the longest cords on the outside edges, attach all cords to the hoop using reverse lark's head knots (see page 11). You should now have 16 reverse lark's head knots with 32 cords.

2 Starting on the outside, take the first and second piece of cord and create a square knot (see page 13). Repeat this process all the way along to create eight square knots.

3 Next, tie a row of seven alternating square knots. Continue making rows of decreasing alternating square knots until you have one single square knot in the middle.

4 Take the last piece of cord on the right-hand side and create reversed double half hitch knots (right), (see page 15) to the centre. Repeat on the left side and join the two pieces together to create a triangle.

5 Cut eight pieces to 30in (76.5cm) and fold in half. Tie all eight cords onto the hoop with reverse lark's head knots. Four on each side of the section you just worked on, working outwards.

6 Take the inside cord on each side and join them together about 1in (2.5cm) below the square knot section. This loop will hold the fringed part of the macramé.

7 To cut the fringe in a 'V' shape, use masking tape to mark your cuts at the bottom. The central piece should measure approximately 12in (30.5cm). Cut diagonally upwards, making the cords shorter as you work outwards. Repeat this same diagonal cut on the other side. This will create the triangle shape at the bottom of the macramé. By doing this first you will have less waste as you can use the excess cord to create the fringing for the next step.

8 Use the trimmings and cut to 8in (20cm) in length – you will need about 20. If you need more, cut them from your cord reel. Take these pieces and make a reverse lark's head knot, adjoining in the middle. Repeat until you have filled from the outer edge to the inner join.

9 To create the central tassel, take five pieces of cord at 14in (35cm) in length and double over the centre part of the tasselled piece. Where they meet, cut the tassel to 5in (13cm). Use a wrap knot (see page 17) to create a tassel here. I like to turn the macramé around and tie this from the back.

10 Brush and trim all the tassels, placing your hand behind the piece to avoid interfering with the macramé at the back. When brushing the cords, make sure you work from the bottom to the top, and with around four cords at a time.

11 Untwist all the bottom ends of the rope to create a frayed look for approximately ½in (1cm) (see page 25). Trim any extra cords to ensure all the ends are the same length. If you don't want to use the masking tape technique to cut, you can use a tape measure to check the length of each strand, working from the inside to the outside.

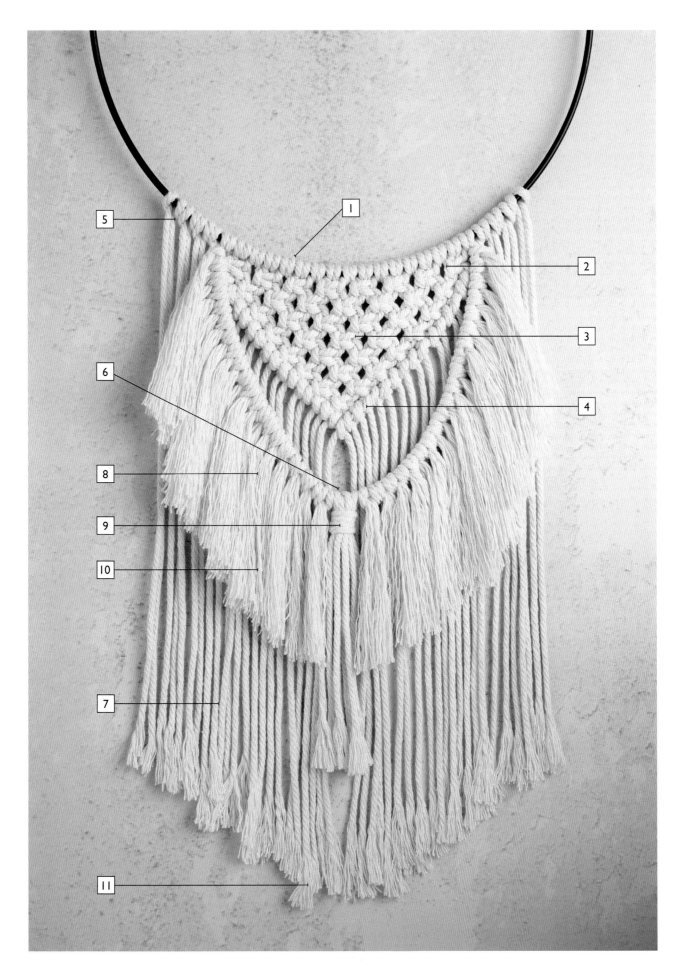

KEYRING

DESIGNED BY FALLON KNOWLES

The pipa knot creates a wonderful shape for a keyring, earring or, if you make it using bigger, chunkier cord, an attractive hanging decoration for around the home.

SKILL LEVEL: REQUIRES EXPERIENCE

YOU'LL NEED

- 19½in (50cm) of ¼in (5mm) braided cotton cord in blue

- Tape measure

- Sharp scissors

KNOTS AND TECHNIQUES

- Pipa knot

- Overhand knot

FINISHED SIZE

Length: 3½in (9cm)

Width: 2in (5cm)

METHOD

1 Lay out the cord vertically on a flat work surface. Create a loop about 2in (5cm) from the end of the cord, to make the top (or neck) of the pipa knot (see page 21). Leave the end piece of cord to one side – this is the non-working cord.

2 Create the bottom loop by making the long piece of cord (working cord) into another loop going clockwise and 2in (5cm) in diameter, crossing the cord over the neck of the pipa knot.

3 Pinch the neck of the two loops together and bring the working cord around the neck at the back, where the top and bottom loops cross over. Bring the working cord back around and down to the bottom loop and follow the inside of the first large loop clockwise with the working cord.

4 Repeat Step 3 by bringing the working cord around the back of the neck of the crossed over cords, and bring the working cord back down and follow the inside of the second loop. Repeat, following the inside of the third loop.

5 Take the working cord for the final time around the back of the knot neck, but instead of creating a loop, pull the cord through the centre of the last loop. Turn the knot over and tie the working cord in securely to the other piece of cord (non-working cord), but don't pull too tight. Either cut the cords short at the back and tuck them under the wrapped-over cord at the back of the pipa knot, or leave them long so that they dangle down.

6 The top loop size can be adjusted by pulling the non-working cord to make the loop smaller before tying a double overhand knot at the back (see page 12).

Tips

This design can be made bigger by making the loop in Step 2 larger. Keep repeating the steps until your bigger loop is filled.

Use an even chunkier cord to create a bigger, bolder pipa knot.

GARLAND

DESIGNED BY ABI WILLIAMS

Gone are the days when bunting was just a party decoration; garlands are now a permanent adornment in many modern homes. From living rooms to hallways, to bedrooms and nurseries, macramé garlands are a simple and fun way of adding both colour and texture to a room.

SKILL LEVEL: EASY

YOU'LL NEED

- 80in (2m) of ⅛in (3mm) braided cord

- 33yd (30m) of ⅛in (3mm) single twist cord in natural

- 22yd (19.5m) of ⅛in (3mm) single twist cord in pink

- 14½yd (13m) of ⅛in (3mm) single twist cord in mustard

- Tape measure

- Sharp scissors

KNOTS AND TECHNIQUES

- Lark's head knot

- Square knot

- Double half hitch knot

- Rya knot

PREPARATION

Cut the following length of braided cord:

1 x 80in (2m)
You can adjust this according to how long you want your garland to be.

Cut the following lengths of natural cord:
30 x 40in (1m)

Cut the following lengths of pink cord:
63 x 12in (30.5cm)

Cut the following lengths of mustard cord:
42 x 12in (30.5cm)

FINISHED SIZE

Length: approximately 6½in (17cm)

Width: approximately 80in (2m), depending on length of cord used

METHOD

1 Attach six lengths of the natural cord to the long piece of braided cord using lark's head knots (see page 11).

2 Tie three square knots (see page 13) along the top row. For the second row, tie two square knots between the top row knots. For the third row, tie one square knot between the second row of knots to make an upside-down triangle shape.

3 Taking the top left cord, create a diagonal line down to the centre point of the triangle using diagonal double half hitch knots (see page 15). Repeat this process starting from the top right cord down to the centre point of the triangle. Join the two rows in the middle using a double half hitch knot. Repeat these steps two more times but leave a small gap between the second and third rows as this is where you will attach the tassels. You will now have a triple outline of the triangle.

4 Using your 12in (30.5cm) long pieces of coloured single twist macramé cord, you will create seven tassels per pennant, three lengths for each tassel. Beginning in the middle, and using rya knots (see page 19), attach the tassels to the garland.

Working outwards to the edge, place your tassels between the last two rows of diagonal double half hitch knots (the last row will be hidden behind the tassels).

5 Repeat Steps 1–4, alternating the colour of the tassels until all five pennants are complete.

6 Trim the tassels to the desired length and shape.

Tips

If you use a cord that is thinner than ⅛in (3mm) single twist macramé cord for the tassels, such as wool, you will probably need to adjust the quantity of lengths per tassel. For example, if you use 1⁄16in (1.5mm) wool, use ten pieces per tassel.

You can customize the length of the garland to be as long or short as you need. You could even make a mini garland using just three pennants to hang under a shelf.

MODERN METAL HANGER

DESIGNED BY EVE WINTER

Adding a metal hoop can completely transform a classic macramé plant hanger into something more captivating and modern.

SKILL LEVEL: REQUIRES EXPERIENCE

YOU'LL NEED

- 12in (30.5cm) metal hoop
- 3in (7cm) diameter wooden dowel ring
- 2in (5cm) diameter wooden dowel ring
- 68yd (62.6m) of ⅛in (3mm) single twist cotton cord in grey
- 4 × ½in (10mm) diameter wooden beads
- Tape measure
- Sharp scissors
- Tapestry needle or crochet hook

PREPARATION

Cut the following lengths of cord:

PLANT HANGER
8 × 7ft (2.2m)
2 × 1½ (50cm)

FRINGE
16 × 8ft (2.5m)
2 × 6½ft (2m)

Feed two 7ft (2.2m) cords through the 3in (7cm) wooden ring. Adjust each cord so that one side is 26in (70cm) long and the other 4¾ft (1.5m). Bundle the four cords together with a loose overhand knot (see page 12) and repeat with the remaining cords.

KNOTS AND TECHNIQUES

- Overhand knot
- Wrap knot
- Crown knot
- Square knot
- Switch knot
- Vertical lark's head knot
- Lark's head knot
- Diagonal double half hitch knot

FINISHED SIZE

Length: approximately 3ft (91cm)

Pot size: approximately 4¼in (11cm) in diameter

METHOD

PLANT HANGER

1 Complete a ¾in (2cm) wrap knot (see page 17) around the cords under the wooden ring.

2 Tie ten rounds of crown knots (see page 24) under the wrap knot.

3 Position the metal hoop under the crown knots. Place two sets of cords in front of the hoop and two sets behind, ensuring that the metal hoop and wooden ring face the same way. Create a ¾in (2cm) wrap knot to secure. Split the cords into four new sets, each containing two working cords and two filler cords. Tie each set with a loose overhand knot (see page 12).

4 Take the first set, and using the shorter cords tie a square knot (see page 13) 3in (7cm) below the wrap knot.

5 Create a switch knot (see page 14) by swapping the working cords with the filler cords and tying another square knot, leaving a ¾in (2cm) gap.

6 Feed a bead onto the filler cords (you may need a crochet hook or tapestry needle to help with this), and secure the bead with a square knot. Create another switch knot with a ¾in (2cm) gap.

7 Repeat Steps 4–6 with the other three sets.

8 Tie four alternating square knots 3in (7cm) below the switch knots to start the net that will hold your pot. Add seven more square knots to each alternating square knot to create a sinnet of eight.

9 Complete the base of the net by attaching the 2in (5cm) wooden dowel ring. Tie a working cord to the ring using a vertical lark's head knot (see page 12), ensuring that the excess cord ends up on the inside of the hanger. Repeat this step with the remaining seven working cords.

10 Secure each pair of vertical lark's head knots by folding the filler cords and holding them against the sinnet on the inside of the hanger. Using the working cords, tie two square knots to enclose the sinnet and the filler cords.

11 Use a crochet hook or tapestry needle to feed each working cord under the new square knots. Pull these tight and cut all loose cords as neatly as possible to complete the first part of the hanger.

FRINGE

1 Fold each of the 8ft (2.5m) cords in half and attach to the bottom of the metal hoop using lark's head knots (see page 11). Attach the two shorter cords to cords 5 and 14.

2 To create the top of the two diamonds, use cord 10 as a filler and tie a row of diagonal double half hitch knots (see page 18), working down and outwards until you reach the edge of the piece. Repeat this on the other side, using cord 27 as a filler. Then take cords 9 and 28 as filler cords (the cords used to create the first two diagonal double half hitch knots), and tie two rows of eight diagonal double half hitch knots down into the centre.

3 Add two more layers of diagonal double half hitch knots to each diamond, ensuring you start with the row that works towards the outside edge each time. Each layer that you create will have one less double half hitch per row. The top of your diamonds should now have three layers, and there should be six working cords per diamond.

4 Tie a square knot in the centre of each diamond. Use the six middle cords as fillers with three working cords either side and create a square knot. Tie a left-facing square knot on the left and a right-facing square knot on the right.

5 To start the bottom half of the diamond, use the three filler cords closest to the outer edge and create three rows of six diagonal double half hitch knots, working down and towards the centre. Repeat on the other side.

6 Using the other working cords, create three rows of diagonal double half hitch knots that work down and away from the centre, right down to the outside edges of the piece. Repeat on the other side. At this point, you should notice a mirrored pattern forming.

7 Create a square knot in the centre of the pattern using the six centre cords as fillers with three working cords each side. This knot will sit between the four diamonds to tie the pattern together.

8 Use the filler cords closest to the middle of the piece to create three more rows of six diagonal double half hitch knots, working down towards the centre of the piece. Repeat on the other side to complete the top half of the second set of diamonds.

9 Repeat Step 4 to create an oversized square knot in the centre of each diamond.

10 To finish the pattern, use the working cords that sit on the inside of the diamond and tie six diagonal double half hitch knots so that they meet. Tie them together using another double half hitch knot, with the cord closest to the outer edge as the working cord. Repeat with the other diamond.

11 Repeat Step 10 for the diamonds' last two rows, adding one diagonal double half hitch knot per row.

12 Trim your fringe. I trimmed it straight to the shortest cord's length, but you could also trim it into a 'V' shape if you wish.

Tip

The key with this piece (and arguably the most challenging part) is to ensure that the vertical lark's head knots are neat and well secured around the top wooden ring. Take your time and pay attention to the detail to make sure that the knots are all the same.

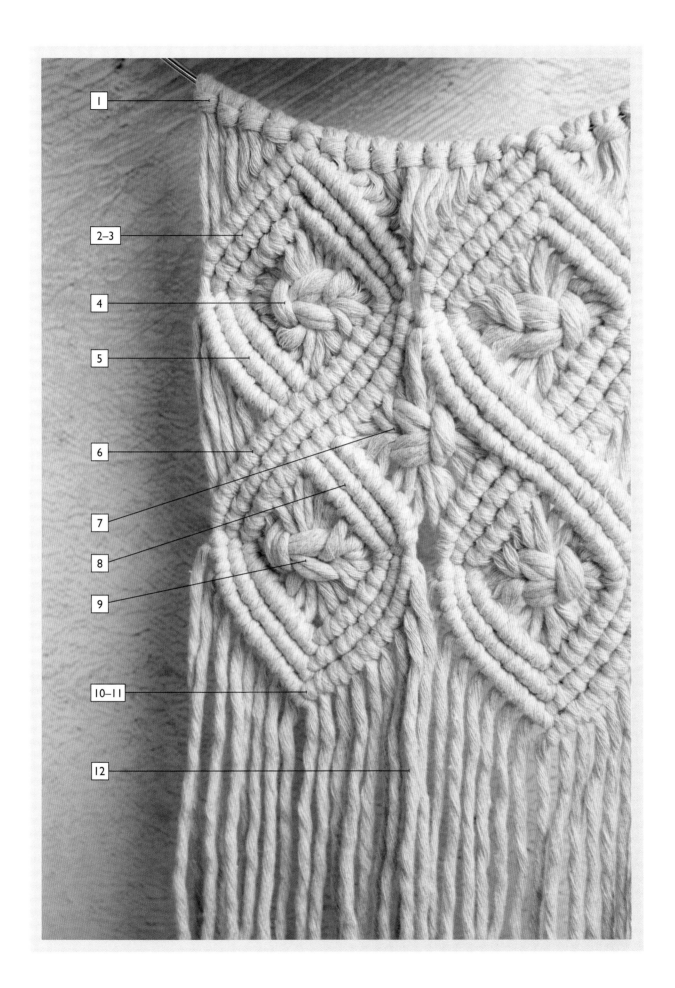

PLACEMAT

DESIGNED BY STEPH BOOTH

Whether indoors or al fresco, these placemats bring decorative texture to the dining experience, also serving the practical purpose of protecting your table top.

SKILL LEVEL: REQUIRES EXPERIENCE

YOU'LL NEED

- Adjustable clothes rail and S-hooks to hang placemat from while you work

- 1½in (1.5cm) thick piece of wooden dowel rod at least 18in (46cm) wide

- 45¾yd (42m) of ⅛in (3mm) 3-ply cotton cord in grey

- 21¾yd (20m) of ⅛in (3mm) 3-ply cotton cord in green

- Tape measure

- Sharp scissors

- Tapestry needle or crochet hook

KNOTS AND TECHNIQUES

- Reverse lark's head knot

- Horizontal double half hitch knot

- Square knot

- Diagonal double half hitch knot

PREPARATION

Cut the following lengths of grey cord:

16 × 8ft (2.5m)
4 × 15½in (39.5cm)

Cut the following lengths of green cord:

8 × 8ft (2.5m)

FINISHED SIZE

Length: 12in (30.5cm)

Width: 17in (43.5cm)

METHOD

1 Attach the dowel rod onto two S-hooks and hang it from the clothes rail. Fold eight of the 8ft (2.5m) grey cords in half and, starting on the left, attach them to the dowel rod using reverse lark's head knots (see page 11). Next, attach the eight 8ft (2.5m) green cords and then the remaining eight 8ft (2.5m) grey cords using reverse lark's head knots.

2 Take one of the 15½in (39.5cm) grey cords and, working from the left of the dowel rod, use it as a filler cord to tie a row of 48 horizontal double half hitch knots (see page 19).

3 Number your cords 1–48. Starting with cords 7–10, tie a square knot (see page 13). Following the increasing square knot pattern, continue to tie rows diagonally directly beneath one another to create a diamond pattern.

4 Repeat Step 3, starting with cords 23–26 and cords 39–42.

5 Drop down ½in (1.5cm) and, starting on the left with cord 1, tie a line of seven diagonal double half hitch knots (see page 18) towards the middle and pointing downwards.

6 Repeat Step 5 starting with cord 16 and work back towards the left.

7 Repeat Steps 5 and 6, tying diagonal double half hitch knots directly beneath.

8 Repeat Steps 5–7 for cords 17–32 and cords 33–48.

9 Starting on the left, take cords 7–10 and tie a square knot directly beneath the diagonal double half hitch knot. Drop down ½in (1cm) and tie a square knot with cords 5–8 and cords 9–12.

10 Repeat Step 9 for cords 21–28 and cords 37–44.

11 Take cords 15–18 and tie a square knot. Drop down ½in (1cm) and, with cords 13–16, tie a square knot, and then with cords 17–20, tie another square knot.

12 Repeat Step 11 for cords 29–36.

13 Repeat Step 2.

14 Starting on the left with cords 1–4, tie two square knots and continue to work across to the right until you have completed the row.

15 Repeat Step 2.

16 Starting on the left, take cords 5–8 and tie a square knot. Repeat for cords 9–12. Drop down ½in (1cm), and with cords 7–10 tie a square knot.

17 Repeat Step 16 for cords 21–28 and 37–44.

18 Take cords 13–20 and drop down ¹⁄₁₆in (1.5cm). Starting with cords 13–16, tie a square knot. Repeat for cords 17–20. Drop down ½in (1cm) and tie a square knot.

19 Repeat Step 18 for cords 29–36.

20 Starting on the left with cord 1, tie a line of seven diagonal double half hitch knots towards the middle and pointing upwards.

21 Repeat Step 20 starting with cord 16 and work back towards the left.

22 Repeat Steps 20 and 21, tying diagonal double half hitch knots directly beneath.

23 Repeat Steps 20, 21 and 22 for cords 17–32 and cords 33–48.

24 Starting with cords 7–10, drop down ¹⁄₁₆in (1.5cm) and tie a square knot. Following the increasing square knot pattern, continue to tie rows diagonally directly beneath one another to create a diamond pattern.

25 Repeat Step 24, starting with cords 23–26 and cords 39–42.

26 Repeat Step 2.

27 Remove the dowel rod and untangle the ends. Cut the ends to make a fringe and repeat for the opposite end, making them the same length.

Tips

The excess cord that you cut at the end of this project can be re-used to create smaller items, such as tassels and hanging decorations.

You can also use any excess trim to create a set of coasters to accompany your placemat project.

FRINGED WALL HANGING

DESIGNED BY FLISS THOMPSON-LEES

The softly brushed fringing of this striking wall hanging contrasts with bold knots and simple shapes to create a variety of layered textures.

SKILL LEVEL: REQUIRES EXPERIENCE

YOU'LL NEED

- Adjustable clothes rail or fixed coat hook to hang piece from while you work

- 10in (25cm) long piece of dowel or wood

- 54½yd (49.9m) of ⅛in (3mm) 4-ply cotton cord in grey

- Tape measure

- Sharp scissors

- Masking tape

- Comb

KNOTS AND TECHNIQUES

- Diagonal double half hitch knot

- Lark's head knot

- Reverse lark's head knot

- Berry knot

- Wrap knot

- Fraying

- Brushing

PREPARATION

Cut a piece of cord 23in (58cm) long and tie it onto the dowel rod using a wrap knot (see page 17). Hang the cord on a wall or rail.

Cut the following lengths of cord:

FRONT PANEL
2 x 3½yd (3.3m)
4 x 60in (91cm)
1 x 10in (25cm)

BACK TASSELS
1 x 18in (46cm)
25 x 39in (1m)

Berry knot section
1 x 13in (33cm)
6 x 20in (51cm)

FINISHED SIZE

Length: approximately 18in (46cm)

Width: approximately 10.5in (27cm)

METHOD

Front panel:

1 Cut two pieces of cord to 3½yd (3.3m), these will be your working cords. Make a reverse lark's head knot (see page 11) to attach these to the dowel at either end.

2 Cut four more pieces of cord to 60in (91cm). Make a reverse lark's head knot either side of the first cords. On each end of the dowel you will have three loops, with the longest in the middle.

3 Starting from the middle make a diagonal line of double half hitch knots (see page 15), working towards the left.

4 Repeat Step 3 in the opposite direction. You should have a triangle shape. Take your working cord and double half hitch knot the next piece, working outwards. You will knot lower than the middle to create a small vertical line, and with one more diagonal double hitch knot you will reach the last piece of cord. Repeat this process on the other side. You should now have an upside-down triangle. Take your working cord and repeat the process backwards to create a diamond shape. Double hitch knot your working cords together and you have made the first diamond shape.

5 Repeat Steps 3–4 five more times. Then repeat it on the other side. You will now have two panels on each end of the wooden dowel with six diamond shapes.

6 Take the last outer piece of cord and make a double hitch knot to join the two panels together. Use the working cord to knot outwards and repeat on the other side to create a small diamond in the centre.

7 Join all the pieces together to start to create your tassel. Use a wrap knot (see page 17) to secure it. Take a piece of cord 10in (25cm) long and work from the back to secure it so you don't see any joins. Wrap the cord around six times. Cut the tassel to 9–10in (22–25cm) and keep the offcuts for later use.

Back tassels:

8 Cut a piece of cord to 18in (46cm) and secure to the wooden dowel with a reverse larks head knot on each side next to front panel. This is the holding cord for the tassels

9 Cut 25 pieces of cord to 39in (1m). Double these up and make a reverse lark's head knot onto the holding cord from step 8. These pieces should hang behind the front panel to give the macramé length. Make sure the tassels are evenly spaced and fill the full length of the holding cord.

Berry knot section:

10 Cut a piece of cord approximately 13in (33cm) and tie it to the wooden dowel with a reverse larks head knot inside the back tassels. This should sit in the centre of your dowel.

11 Cut six pieces of cord to 20in (51cm). Fold in half and add to the cord for this berry knot section, attached to the dowel. Make a reverse lark's head knot to secure. This berry knot section should sit in the middle of the front panel and back tassel sections.

12 You now have 12 cords. Starting from the left, take the first four cords and make a berry knot (see page 16). Repeat with all the cords. You now have a row of three berry knots.

13 Trim back tassels to required length. Work from the middle outwards to create a diagonal line. (I use diagonally placed masking tape to help with my lines.) Work from 18in (46cm) outwards, reducing the length. Cut a gradual diagonal line end piece around 15in (38cm).

14 Return to the front panel and use 28 pieces of cord 7in (18cm) long. These will be attached to the front panel to create the fringing. Attach these along the front panel, making a reverse larks head knot between the pattern. Attach evenly from the top to the middle knot.

15 Once all the cord is attached, gently brush (see page 25) each piece. Place your hand behind to avoid disturbing the back tassels. Brush each section from bottom to top, then trim to even out any unevenness.

16 Gently fray (see page 25) the bottom part of the back tassels and also the bottom of your tassel.

Tips

This project may look a little complicated, but once you've mastered the diagonal double hitch knot, it's actually quite easy. The wall hanging can be made in other colours, and it can be scaled up to create bigger pieces. Also, you can replace the dowel rod with a branch to create a different look and feel.

14–15

13

16

RESOURCES

Cord

Amazon - amazon.com
Anchor Crafts – anchorcrafts.com
Bobbiny – bobbiny.com
Rope Source – rope-source.co.uk

Haberdashery and basic equipment

Amazon – amazon.com
Dannells – dannells.com
Hobbycraft – hobbycraft.co.uk
John Lewis – johnlewis.com

DESIGNER INFORMATION

To find out more about the designers featured in this book, visit their Instagram profiles listed below:

Lucy Booth
@fibreartsandco

Steph Booth
@boothie_makesandbakes

Fallon Knowles
@fallonknowles

Sarah Lavinay
@cotswold_crafts_by_saya

Hannah McVie
@homely_knots

Lisa Miller
@literallyknot

Tabitha Morgan-Earp
@morganmacrame

Isabella Strambio
@_twome

Fliss Thompson-Lees
@loubelle__

Abi Williams
@wooliamsmacrame

Eve Winter
@cottonandcorduk

INDEX

To order a book, contact:

GMC Publications Ltd
Castle Place, 166 High Street,
Lewes, East Sussex,
BN7 1XU
United Kingdom
Tel: +44 (0)1273 488005
www.gmcbooks.com